KODOKAN JUDO

PROF. JIGORO KANO

KODOKAN JUDO

Jigoro Kano

Edited under the supervision of
the Kodokan Editorial Committee

KODANSHA INTERNATIONAL
Tokyo • New York • London

Distributed in the United States by Kodansha America, Inc., 114
Fifth Avenue, New York, N.Y. 10011, and in the United Kingdom
and continental Europe by Kodansha Europe Ltd., 95 Aldwych,
London WC2B 4JF. Published by Kodansha International Ltd.,
17-14 Otowa 1-chome, Bunkyo-ku, Tokyo 112, and Kodansha
America, Inc. Copyright © 1986 by Kodansha International Ltd.
All rights reserved. Printed in Japan.
First edition, 1986
First paperback edition, 1994
97 98 99 00 10 9 8 7 6 5
                                            LCC-8480160
                                       ISBN 4-7700-1799-5

Contributors

Yoshitsugu Yamashita, 10th *dan*[†]
Hajime Isogai, 10th *dan*[†]
Shuichi Nagaoka, 10th *dan*[†]
Kyuzo Mifune, 10th *dan*[†]
Kaichiro Samura, 10th *dan*[†]
Sumiyuki Kotani, 10th *dan*
Yoshizo Matsumoto, 9th *dan*
Teizo Kawamura, 9th *dan*
Toshiro Daigo, 9th *dan*
Yoshimi Osawa, 9th *dan*
Saburo Matsushita, 8th *dan*
Shiro Yamamoto, 8th *dan*
Tsuyoshi Sato, 8th *dan*
Kazuhiko Kawabe, 7th *dan*
Jiro Miura, 7th *dan*
Hiroshi Onozawa, 7th *dan*

Haruko Niboshi, 7th *dan*
Naoko Miyajima, 6th *dan*
Katsuko Umezu, 6th *dan*
Keiko Ishibashi, 6th *dan*
Sumiko Akiyama, 6th *dan*

Note: [†]indicates the person is deceased. The last five names are those of women judoka.

The Kodokan International Judo Center

Contents

V HEALTH AND FIRST AID

Foreword

To speak of judo is to speak of Jigoro Kano. To hear the name of Jigoro Kano is to be reminded of the Kodokan.

In 1982, the Kodokan entered its hundredth year of vigorous activity, for it was in February, 1882, that Kodokan Judo came into existence and three months later, in May, that the Kodokan was established.

To celebrate the great achievements of Jigoro Kano and to create fresh momentum for the promotion and realization of his ideals, numerous commemorative events are being held under the auspices of the Kodokan. One of these, the grand opening ceremony of the new main dojo, took place in April, 1984, to mark the centenary of the Kodokan and the completion of the new Kodokan International Judo Center.

Professor Kano aimed at human perfection through judo and the betterment of mankind in the spirit of mutual prosperity. This lofty ideal is at the heart of the Kodokan philosophy and its realization has been pursued unceasingly from the very beginning, and will without doubt continue to be pursued in the future throughout the world.

This book, being published as one of these events, is a new edition of the original work compiled and edited by Professor Kano's former students and followers and first published in 1956. The original work consisted of his teachings concerning the theory and techniques of judo. In this new edition, the original is supplemented by other writings of Professor Kano, as well as by demonstrations and explanations of leading experts.

The 1956 edition is an invaluable historical document that has come to be regarded as the unrivaled source book on judo. Published under the imprint of the Kodokan, it is regarded as the definitive work for the teaching of judo and its prestige is without equal in any country. Naturally, there have been frequent demands for its reprinting, but eventually this became impossible. This new revised edition of *Kodokan Judo*, therefore, is being offered in response to numerous requests heard both in Japan and abroad.

Recent years have seen the astounding internationalization of judo. At the same time, there has been a tendency everywhere for certain changes to creep in. In this connection, the question "What is judo?" is highly relevant and deserves an answer.

As clearly stated in Paragraph I of the Regulations of the International Judo Federation, "It [I.J.F.] recognizes as judo that which was created by

Jigoro Kano." From the viewpoint of the correct dissemination of judo throughout the world, it is highly desirable that the real meaning and nature of judo, as given in this book, be recognized.

It is my sincere wish that, as this important book makes its timely appearance, it will be read throughout the world not only by those who teach, but by all who practice and enjoy judo.

Yukimitsu Kano
President, Kodokan

Note: As indicated above, this book is a revision of *Kodokan Judo*, published in 1956. The present volume incorporates additional material from three sources. Chapter 1, paragraphs 1 through 5 of chapter 2 and paragraphs 1 through 3 of chapter 3 were composed in English by Professor Jigoro Kano. These sections appeared in a book called *Judo (Jujutsu)* published in 1937 by the Maruzen Company (Tokyo). Another section was written in Japanese by Professor Kano and is here translated as the last section of chapter 2. This was published by Hori Shoten (Tokyo) in September, 1931, in *Judo Kyohon*. Other parts of the present work were written by the Kodokan editorial committee so that the will and spirit of the author might be preserved and presented to judo students the world over.

The contributors to this book are listed on page 5. In addition it should be noted that the *tori* in Koshiki no Kata is Jigoro Kano and the *uke* is Yoshitsugu Yamashita.

I
BASIC JUDO CONCEPTS

1. Jujutsu Becomes Judo

1. The cradle of Kodokan judo. This is the main gate of the Buddhist temple Eishoji.

Most people are no doubt familiar with the words *jujutsu* and *judo*, but how many can distinguish between them? Here, I will explain the two terms and tell why *judo* came to take the place of *jujutsu*.

Many martial arts were practiced in Japan during its feudal age: the use of the lance, archery, swordsmanship and many more. Jujutsu was one such art. Also called *taijutsu* and *yawara*, it was a system of attack that involved throwing, hitting, kicking, stabbing, slashing, choking, bending and twisting limbs, pinning an opponent, and defenses against these attacks. Although jujutsu's techniques were known from the earliest times, it was not until the latter half of the sixteenth century that jujutsu was practiced and taught systematically. During the Edo period (1603–1868) it developed

2. The creation of judo is commemorated by a memorial stone in the garden of the Eishoji.

3. Techniques of the Tenshin Shin'yo School of jujutsu are one of the sources of judo techniques.

into a complex art taught by the masters of a number of schools.

In my youth I studied jujutsu under many eminent masters. Their vast knowledge, the fruit of years of diligent research and rich experience, was of great value to me. At that time, each man presented his art as a collection of techniques. None perceived the guiding principle behind jujutsu. When I encountered differences in the teaching of techniques, I often found myself at a loss to know which was correct. This led me to look for an underlying principle in jujutsu, one that applied when one hit an opponent as well as when one threw him. After a thorough study of the subject, I discerned an all-pervasive principle: to make the most efficient use of mental and physical energy. With this principle in mind, I again reviewed all the methods of attack and defense I had learned, retaining only those that were in accordance with the principle. Those not in accord with it I rejected, and in their place I substituted techniques in which the principle was correctly applied. The resulting body of technique, which I named judo to distinguish it from its predecessor, is what is taught at the Kodokan.

The words *jujutsu* and *judo* are each written with two Chinese characters. The *ju* in both is the same and means "gentleness" or "giving way." The meaning of *jutsu* is "art, practice," and *do* means "principle" or "way," the Way being the concept of life itself. Jujutsu may be translated as "the gentle art," *judo* as "the Way of gentleness," with the implication of first giving way to ultimately gain victory. The Kodokan is, literally, "the school for studying the Way." As we shall see in the next chapter, judo is more than an art of attack and defense. It is a way of life.

To understand what is meant by *gentleness* or *giving way*, let us say a man is standing before me whose strength is ten, and that my own strength is but

4. Using the principle of *yawara*, even a small person can throw a large one.

5. A defenseless woman can nullify the strength of a giant if she uses her own power effectively.

seven. If he pushes me as hard as he can, I am sure to be pushed back or knocked down, even if I resist with all my might. This is opposing strength with strength. But if instead of opposing him I give way to the extent he has pushed, withdrawing my body and maintaining my balance, my opponent will lose his balance. Weakened by his awkward position, he will be unable to use all his strength. It will have fallen to three. Because I retain my balance, my strength remains at seven. Now I am stronger than my opponent and can defeat him by using only half my strength, keeping the other half available for some other purpose. Even if you are stronger than your opponent, it is better first to give way. By doing so you conserve energy while exhausting your opponent.

This is but one example of how you can defeat an opponent by giving way.

6. Judo training at the Fujimi-cho dojo as depicted by Shuzan Hishida. Observing from the platform at left is Master Kano.

It was because so many techniques made use of this principle that the art was named jujutsu. Let us look at a few other examples of the feats that can be accomplished with jujutsu.

Suppose a man is standing before me. Like a log on end, he can be pushed off balance—frontward or backward—with a single finger. If at the moment he leans forward, I apply my arm to his back and quickly slip my hip in front of his, my hip becomes a fulcrum. To throw the man to the ground, even if he greatly outweighs me, all I need do is twist my hip slightly or pull on his arm or sleeve.

Let us say I attempt to break a man's balance to the front, but that he steps forward with one foot. I can still throw him easily by merely pressing the ball of my foot just below the Achilles' tendon of his advancing leg a split second before he places his full weight on that foot. This is a good example of the efficient use of energy. With only slight effort, I can defeat an opponent of considerable strength.

What if a man were to rush up and push me? If instead of pushing back, I were to take hold of his arms or his collar with both hands, place the ball of one foot against his lower abdomen, straighten my leg and sit back, I could make him somersault over my head.

Or suppose that my opponent leans forward a bit and pushes me with one hand. This puts him off balance. If I grab him by the upper sleeve of his outstretched arm, pivot so that my back is close to his chest, clamp my free hand on his shoulder and suddenly bend over, he will go flying over my head and land flat on his back.

As these examples show, for the purpose of throwing an opponent the principle of leverage is sometimes more important than giving way. Jujutsu also includes other forms of direct attack, such as hitting, kicking and chok-

7. Master Kano gives instruction in judo to foreign trainees at the University of Berlin, 1933.

ing. In this respect, the "art of giving way" does not convey the true meaning. If we accept jujutsu as the art or practice of making the most efficient use of mental and physical energy, then we can think of judo as the way, the principle, of doing this, and we arrive at a true definition.

In 1882 I founded the Kodokan to teach judo to others. Within a few years, the number of students rapidly increased. They came from all over Japan, many having left jujutsu masters to train with me. Eventually judo displaced jujutsu in Japan, and no one any longer speaks of jujutsu as a contemporary art in Japan, although the word has survived overseas.

2. Principles and Aims of Kodokan Judo

JUDO AS PHYSICAL EDUCATION

Encouraged by my success in applying the principle of maximum efficiency to the techniques of attack and defense, I then asked if the same principle could not be applied to the improvement of health, that is, to physical education.

Many opinions have been advanced to answer the question, what is the aim of physical education? After giving the matter a great deal of thought and exchanging views with many knowledgeable persons, I concluded that its aim is making the body strong, useful and healthy while building character through mental and moral discipline. Having thus clarified the purpose of physical education, let us see how closely the common methods of physical education conform to the principle of maximum efficiency.

The ways in which persons train their bodies are many and varied, but they fall into two general categories: sports and gymnastics. It is difficult to generalize about sports, since there are so many different types, but they share one important characteristic: they are competitive in nature. The objective in devising them has not been to foster balanced physical development or sound health. Inevitably some muscles are consistently overworked while others are neglected. In the process, damage is sometimes done to various areas of the body. As physical education, many sports cannot be rated highly—in fact, should be discarded or improved—for they fail to make the most efficient use of mental and physical energy and impede progress toward the goal of promoting health, strength and usefulness.

By contrast, gymnastics rate highly as physical education. Practice is not injurious to the body, is generally beneficial to health, and promotes the balanced development of the body. Still, gymnastics as commonly practiced today are lacking in two respects: interest and usefulness.

There are many ways in which gymnastics can be made more appealing, but one that I advocate is to do a group of exercises I have tentatively worked out. Each combination of limb, neck and body movements is based on the principle of maximum efficiency and represents an idea. Done in combination, they will effectively promote harmonious physical and moral development. Another set of exercises I created, the *Seiryoku Zen'yo Kokumin Taiiku* (Maximum-Efficiency National Physical Education), is practiced at the Kodokan. Its movements not only lead to balanced physical development but also provide training in the basics of attack and defense. I have written about this in complete detail in chapter 19.

For physical education to be truly effective, it must be based on the principle of efficient use of mental and physical energy. I am convinced that

1. A hanging scroll with the calligraphy, "Maximum-efficient use of power," written by Master Kano. *Power* means both physical strength and mental power.

future advances in physical education will be made in conformity with this principle.

TWO METHODS OF TRAINING

So far I have touched on the two main aspects of judo training: development of the body and training in the forms of attack and defense. The primary training methods for either purpose are (1) *kata* and (2) *randori*.

Kata, which means "form," is a system of prearranged movements that teach the fundamentals of attack and defense. In addition to throwing and holding (also practiced in randori), it includes hitting, kicking, stabbing,

2. Women training in *kata* at the Kodokan.

slashing and a number of other techniques. These latter occur only in kata because it is only in kata that the movements are prearranged and each partner knows what the other will do.

Randori means "free practice." Partners pair off and vie with each other as they would in an actual match. They may throw, pin, choke and apply joint locks, but they may not hit, kick or employ other techniques appropriate only to actual combat. The main conditions in randori are that participants take care not to injure each other and that they follow judo etiquette, which is mandatory if one is to derive the maximum benefit from randori.

Randori may be practiced either as training in the methods of attack and defense or as physical education. In either case, all movements are made in conformity with the principle of maximum efficiency. If training in attack and defense is the objective, concentration on the proper execution of techniques is sufficient. But beyond that, randori is ideal for physical culture, since it involves all parts of the body, and unlike gymnastics, all its movements are purposeful and executed with spirit. The objective of this systematic physical training is to perfect control over mind and body and to prepare a person to meet any emergency or attack, accidental or intentional.

TRAINING THE MIND

Both kata and randori are forms of mental training, but of the two, randori is the more effective.

In randori, one must search out the opponent's weaknesses and be ready to attack with all the resources at his disposal the moment the opportunity presents itself, without violating the rules of judo. Practicing randori tends to make the student earnest, sincere, thoughtful, cautious and deliberate in action. At the same time, he or she learns to value and make quick decisions and to act promptly, for, whether attacking or defending, there is no place in randori for indecisiveness.

In randori one can never be sure what technique the opponent will employ next, so he must be constantly on guard. Being alert becomes second nature. One acquires poise, the self-confidence that comes from knowing that he can cope with any eventuality. The powers of attention and observation, imagination, of reasoning and judgement are naturally heightened, and these are all useful attributes in daily life as well as in the dojo.

To practice randori is to investigate the complex mental-physical relations existing between contestants. Hundreds of valuable lessons are derivable from this study.

In randori we learn to employ the principle of maximum efficiency even when we could easily overpower an opponent. Indeed, it is much more impressive to beat an opponent with proper technique than with brute force. This lesson is equally applicable in daily life: the student realizes that persuasion backed up by sound logic is ultimately more effective than coercion.

Another tenet of randori is to apply just the right amount of force—never too much, never too little. All of us know of people who have failed to accomplish what they set out to do because of not properly gauging the amount of effort required. At one extreme, they fall short of the mark; at the other, they do not know when to stop.

In randori we occasionally come up against an opponent who is frantic in his desire to win. We are trained not to resist directly with force but to play with the opponent until his fury and power are exhausted, then attack. This lesson comes in handy when we encounter such a person in daily life. Since no amount of reasoning will have any effect on him, all we can do is wait for him to calm down.

These are but a few examples of the contributions randori can make to the intellectual training of young minds.

ETHICAL TRAINING

Let us now look at the ways in which an understanding of the principle of maximum efficiency constitutes ethical training.

There are people who are excitable by nature and allow themselves to become angry for the most trivial of reasons. Judo can help such people learn to control themselves. Through training, they quickly realize that anger is a waste of energy, that it has only negative effects on the self and others.

Training in judo is also extremely beneficial to those who lack confidence in themselves due to past failures. Judo teaches us to look for the best possible course of action, whatever the individual circumstances, and helps us to understand that worry is a waste of energy. Paradoxically, the man who has failed and one who is at the peak of success are in exactly the same position. Each must decide what he will do next, choose the course that will lead

3. Training in *randori* at the Kodokan.

him to the future. The teachings of judo give each the same potential for success, in the former instance guiding a man out of lethargy and disappointment to a state of vigorous activity.

One more type who can benefit from the practice of judo are the chronically discontented, who readily blame others for what is really their own fault. These people come to realize that their negative frame of mind runs counter to the principle of maximum efficiency and that living in conformity with the principle is the key to a forward-looking mental state.

AESTHETICS

Practicing judo brings many pleasures: the pleasant feeling exercise imparts to muscles and nerves, the satisfaction of mastering movements, and the joy of winning in competition. Not the least of these is the beauty and delight of performing graceful, meaningful techniques and in seeing others perform them. This is the essence of the aesthetic side of judo.

JUDO OUTSIDE THE DOJO

Contests in judo have as their rationale the idea that the lessons taught in matches will find application not only in future training but in the world at large. Here I would like to point out five basic principles and show briefly how they operate in the social realm.

First is the maxim which says that one should pay close attention to the relationship between self and other. To take an example, before making an attack, one should note his opponent's weight, build, strong points, temperament and so on. He should be nonetheless aware of his own strengths and weaknesses, and his eye should critically assess his surroundings. In the days when matches were held outdoors, he would inspect the area for such things as rocks, ditches, walls and the like. In the dojo, he takes note of walls, people or other potential obstructions. If a person has carefully observed everything, then the correct means of defeating an opponent will naturally become apparent.

The second point has to do with taking the lead. Players of board games like chess and *go* are familiar with the strategy of making a move that will entice the other player to move in a certain way. This concept is clearly applicable to both judo and our daily lives.

Stated succinctly, the third point is: Consider fully, act decisively. The first phrase is closely related to the first point above, that is, a man should meticulously evaluate his adversary before executing a technique. This done, the advice given in the second phrase is followed automatically. To act decisively means to do so without hesitation and without second thoughts.

Having shown how to proceed, I would now like to advise you when to stop. This can be stated quite simply. When a predetermined point has been reached, it is time to cease applying the technique, or whatever.

The fifth and final point evokes the very essence of judo. It is contained in the saying: Walk a single path, becoming neither cocky with victory nor broken with defeat, without forgetting caution when all is quiet or becoming frightened when danger threatens. Implicit here is the admonition that if we let ourselves be carried away by success, defeat will inevitably follow victory. It also means that one should always be prepared for a contest—even the moment after scoring a victory. Whether a person's surroundings are calm or turbulent, he should always exploit whatever means are at hand to accomplish his purpose.

The student of judo should bear these five principles in mind. Applied in the work place, the school, the political world or any other area of society, he will find that the benefits are great.

To sum up, judo is a mental and physical discipline whose lessons are readily applicable to the management of our daily affairs. The fundamental principle of judo, one that governs all the techniques of attack and defense, is that whatever the objective, it is best attained by the maximum-efficient use of mind and body for that purpose. The same principle applied to our everyday activities leads to the highest and most rational life.

Training in the techniques of judo is not the only way to grasp this universal principle, but it is how I arrived at an understanding of it, and it is the means by which I attempt to enlighten others.

The principle of maximum efficiency, whether applied to the art of attack and defense or to refining and perfecting daily life, demands above all that there be order and harmony among people. This can be realized only through mutual aid and concession. The result is mutual welfare and benefit. The final aim of judo practice is to inculcate respect for the principles of maximum efficiency and mutual welfare and benefit. Through judo, persons individually and collectively attain their highest spiritual state while at the same time developing their bodies and learning the art of attack and defense.

3. Basic Points in Training

1. The main dojo of the Kodokan International Judo Center, completed in 1984.

THE DOJO

Judo is practiced in a specially designed building known as a *dojo*. The practice area is devoid of sharp corners and potentially dangerous obstructions, such as pillars, and walls are often paneled. The floor of the room is covered with reinforced mats, their size and shape being the same as the tatami found in homes. The mats absorb the impact of falls. To avoid foot injuries, great care is taken to see that the mats are laid flat, without spaces between them. Torn mats must be promptly repaired or replaced.

When visiting a dojo for the first time, one is likely to notice how clean it is kept and to be impressed by its solemn atmosphere. We should remember that the word *dojo* comes from a Buddhist term referring to the "place of enlightenment." Like a monastery, the dojo is a sacred place to which people come to perfect body and mind.

Randori and kata practice are done in the dojo, which is also the place where matches are held.

2. The judogi with the belt properly tied as seen from the front.

3. The judogi as seen from the back.

THE JUDOGI

The jacket, pants and belt worn when practicing judo are collectively called *judogi*. The jacket and pants are white; the belt varies in color according to the rank of the wearer.

Beginners, who hold no rank, wear white belts. Boys ranking third *kyu* (class) through first *kyu* wear violet belts; adults, brown belts. Those who rank from first *dan* (grade) through fifth *dan* wear black belts. From sixth through eighth *dan* the belt has red-and-white stripes. Ninth *dan* and above wear a red belt. Holders of the sixth *dan* and above may, however, wear black belts if they prefer. Women's belts have a white stripe down the middle.

Figs. 2 and *3* show, respectively, the front and back of the judogi.

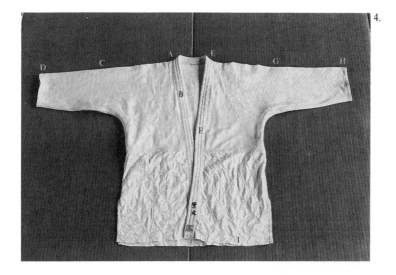

4.

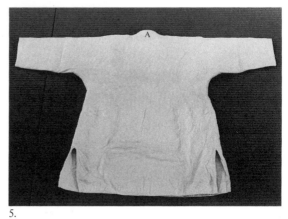

5.

4. Judogi jacket, front.
   A. Right side collar
   B. Right front collar
   C. Right middle outer sleeve
   D. Right lower outer sleeve
   E. Left side collar
   F. Left front collar
   G. Left middle outer sleeve
   H. Left lower outer sleeve
   I. Jacket bottom

5. Judogi jacket, back
   A. Back collar

6. Judogi pants
   A. Belt
   B. Right front leg
   C. Left front leg

6.

7.

8.

9.

10.

11.

14.

12.

13.

Putting on the judogi

7. Put the jacket on in the normal way, left side folded over right side.

8. Extend the center of the belt across the abdomen at waist level.

9. Bring the ends around your back and out to the front.

10. Begin the knot by crossing one end of the belt over the other end.

11. Pass one end of the belt between the back of the belt and the jacket.

12–13. Finish tying the knot.

14. Tie a flat reef or double square knot. Make it as flat and tight as possible.

15.

16.

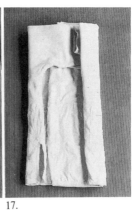

17.

18.

19.

Folding the judogi

15. Place the pants on top of the jacket.
16. Fold the sleeves in.
17–18. Fold the sides of the jacket and the pants inward, then do this a second time.
19. Fold the top over the bottom.
20. The belt can be used to tie the folded judgogi into a bundle.

20.

ETIQUETTE IN THE DOJO

Before and after practicing judo or engaging in a match, opponents bow to each other. Bowing is an expression of gratitude and respect. In effect, you are thanking your opponent for giving you the opportunity to improve your technique.

Bowing is done either sitting or standing.

To perform a sitting bow, opponents sit on bent knees facing each other about 1.5 meters apart, insteps flush with the mat, knees slightly apart, hips resting on heels, hands on thighs. (*Fig. 21*) The hands are then placed on the mat 10 to 12 centimeters in front of the knees, with the fingertips turned slightly inward. Bow from the waist with the head and neck forming a straight line with the back. (*Fig. 22*)

21.

22.

23. Rear view shows how feet are placed when taking this formal sitting position, which is called *seiza*.

24.

25.

26. Members of a Kodokan boys' class sit in the formal style as part of their training.

For the standing bow, opponents come to attention about 2 meters apart. (*Fig. 24*) Then they bend forward from the waist, letting their hands move from the sides to the front of their legs, until their bodies form approximately a 30-degree angle. (*Fig. 25*)

The sitting bow is the more formal of the two. It is always done before and after practicing kata. The standing bow is made to one's instructors and seniors when entering and leaving the dojo. Before and after randori one may do a standing bow or an abbreviated form of the sitting bow in which the toes and heels are slightly raised.

Depending on the circumstances, opponents may bow from greater distances, but they must always show sincerity.

In other ways, too, students of judo are expected to exhibit proper decorum in the dojo. The dojo is not the place for idle talk or frivolous behavior. In practice or in a match, students should go all out, and when resting they should watch others practice; by doing so they may learn something. Eating, drinking and smoking are not tolerated in the dojo, and students are urged to keep it neat and clean.

Personal hygiene is also important. Students should be clean and keep their fingernails and toenails short to avoid injuring others. The judogi should be washed regularly and any tears mended promptly. To get the most out of training, one should always practice moderation in eating, drinking and sleeping.

THE IMPORTANCE OF REGULAR PRACTICE

Students sometimes err in their training by practicing either too much or too little. Insufficient practice is the more common problem.

The real value of judo only appears as a result of regular practice. To derive the maximum physical, mental and spiritual benefits from judo, one should practice every day without fail. On those days when it is impossible to train in the dojo, one should as a minimum perform the Seiryoku Zen'yo Kokumin Taiiku.

A WORD OF CAUTION

In the early stages of judo training, students, especially young people, sometimes feel tempted to try out their newly learned techniques on unsuspecting persons. Such behavior is irresponsible and highly dangerous. One must never misuse judo teechniques, for this can result in serious injury or even death. And needless to say, it goes against the spirit of judo. The only time one is justified in applying judo techniques outside the dojo is when in immediate physical danger.

27. Boys practice the fundamentals at the Kodokan.

28–29. Practice in defensive skills is the most basic of all judo training.

By resorting to inappropriate behavior, a person places himself in grave danger. If he has not hesitated to experiment on others, he is hardly in a position to blame anyone who attempts to try something out on him. He is bound to run into stronger individuals and there is no knowing what may happen. Attacked when off guard or even asleep, no one stands much of a chance, even against a weaker assailant. Outside of training, it is forbidden to try out the techniques one has learned.

On the folly of misusing the knowledge one acquires through training in judo, the following is a story that has come down to us from the past.

A certain student, eager to test his techniques, would go out each evening to a lonely spot along the road, and there would lie in wait for the occasional passerby. When someone happened along he would spring out and apply one of his throws.

Eventually word of the man's actions reached his teacher. Disguising himself, the teacher went to the spot one evening. The student, not recognizing his teacher, rushed out and attacked as usual. The teacher allowed himself to be thrown, then slowly stood up and told the student to examine his side. Realizing who the man was, the student quickly looked down. There on his right side he saw a streak of grease that his teacher had applied while being thrown, indicating that he could easily have killed the student with an *atemi* blow. Humbled by his experience, the student never again ventured out to test his throws on innocent passersby.

II
TECHNIQUES

4. Basic Movements

POSTURES

Shizen Hontai
Basic Natural Posture

1. The basic judo posture is taken by standing naturally, heels about 30 centimeters apart, arms in a relaxed position at the sides.

Migi/Hidari Shizentai
Right/Left Natural Posture

2. Stand with one foot 30 centimeters forward.

Jigo Hontai
Basic Defensive Posture

3. Stand with your feet about 75 centimeters apart and bend your knees to lower your center of gravity.

Migi/Hidari Jigotai
Right/Left Defensive Posture

4. Stand with one foot about 70 centimeters forward and bend your knees.

THE BASIC HOLD

The basic hold is the same, whatever the posture. Your grip should be loose enough so that you can change holds quickly if necessary. If there is a time lag in changing grips, the opponent can take advantage of this for a counter move. After mastering use of the basic hold in all throws, experiment with other holds. It will be found that some work better for some throws than others.

5. Taking the basic hold in the right natural posture.

6. Taking the basic hold in the right defensive posture.

7. Hold the opponent's left lapel at the armpit level with your right hand and his right outer sleeve near the elbow with your left.

MOVING AND TURNING

Movement forward, backward or to the sides is called *shintai*.

When moving in any direction, the feet are slid across the mat with most of one's weight over the leading foot. The natural walking style is called *ayumi-ashi*. More common when close to an opponent is the style called *tsugi-ashi*. (*Figs. 8–10*) In *tsugi-ashi*, whether you move forward, backward, sideways or diagonally, one foot always leads and the other follows. After each step one assumes one of the basic postures. Steps should not be too large and the feet are never brought together.

Tai-sabaki is the term for body control. This involves primarily turning movements, which must be fluid and fast. The body must be carried lightly and you must maintain your balance at all times. Mastery of *tai-sabaki* is the key to executing effective throwing techniques. *Figs. 11–15* show the five basic types.

8. *Tsugi-ashi 1*: forward and backward.

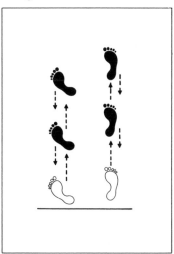

9. *Tsugi-ashi 2*: sideways.

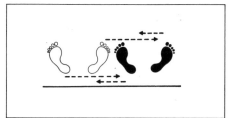

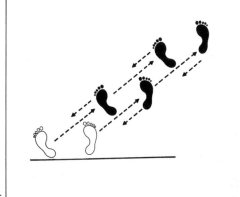

10. *Tsugi-ashi 3*: diagonally.

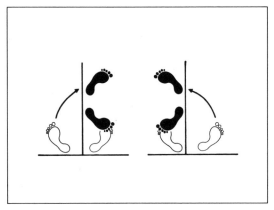

11. *Tai-sabaki 1*: Advancing one foot, turn to face in the direction of the other (pivot) foot.

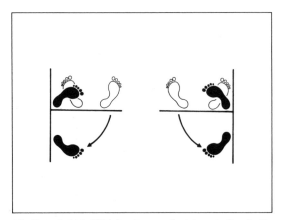

12. *Tai-sabaki 2*: Withdrawing one foot, turn to face in the direction of the other (pivot) foot.

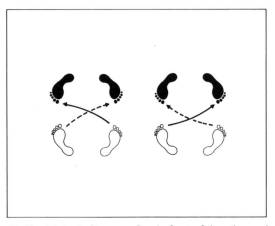

13. *Tai-sabaki 3*: Cross one foot in front of the other and pivot backward to reverse direction.

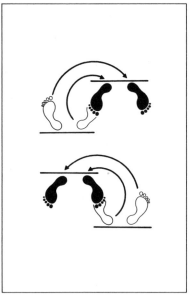

14. *Tai-sabaki 4*: Pivot on the ball of one foot and turn forward to reverse direction.

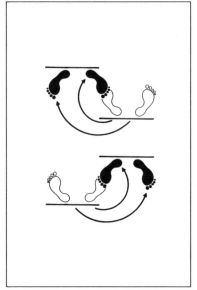

15. *Tai-sabaki 5*: Pivot on the ball of one foot and turn backward to reverse direction.

THE PRINCIPLE OF DYNAMICS

The diagrams below show what is important in terms of dynamics and the body's center of gravity. Best results are ensured by making use of the opponent's strength. On your part, composure, rather than mere strength, is important to keep muscles and joints from stiffening. Especially in emergencies, body strength should be conserved, then applied at the correct moment.

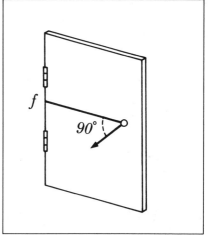

17. A heavy door can be moved with ease because we apply pressure at a right angle to its surface at a point well removed from the door's fulcrum (*f*), which is the hinged side.

16. A person is balanced as long as the vertical gravitational line passes through the middle of the base formed by his legs and hips. When it does not, he is off balance and can be brought down with moderate effort.

18. To the front.

20. To the left.

19. To the back.

21. To the right.

Kuzushi

To use strength most efficiently, it is vital to break the opponent's balance. In line with the principle of dynamics, he is then vulnerable and can be brought down with a minimum of effort. Breaking an opponent's balance is called *kuzushi*. With reference to the basic natural posture, it has eight forms as illustrated here.

The basis of kuzushi is pushing and pulling, which are done with the whole body, not just the arms. At times this involves more than just a push

22. To the right front corner.

24. To the right back corner.

23. To the left front corner.

25. To the left back corner.

or a pull. One may, for instance, push and let go, push and let go, or push and then pull, or pull and then push. Kuzushi can be done in either straight or curved lines and in every direction. Learning all eight basic forms and using them in combinations is indispensable to fundamental judo techniques.

In countering your opponent's attempt to break your balance, give way to him, then apply your own kuzushi. If pushed, go with the force of the push while maintaining your balance, then pull. This will cause your opponent to lose his balance. If pulled, push.

26–27. Master Kano demonstrates judo techniques.

Tsukuri and *Kake*

To execute a throw (*kake*), after breaking your opponent's balance you must move your body into position for the throw. This is known as *tsukuri*. If your opponent is weaker than you, you may be able to throw him without good tsukuri, but you may cause injury. Furthermore, without good tsukuri you will be unable to throw opponents who are stronger than you. Beginners should therefore concentrate on mastering tsukuri and should polish kake later. It is also necessary to know how to hold oneself in readiness for the attack.

Falling Backward

28.

29.

30.

31.

32.

33.

From a sitting position

28. Sit upright with your legs forward and your arms stretched out at shoulder height, palms down.

29–30. Fall backward, curving your back and raising your legs.

31. Tuck in your chin and slap the mat hard with your hands and arms the moment your back meets the mat. The arms should be at a 30–45-degree angle from the body.

32. Sit up by lowering your legs.

33. Return to your original position.

Ukemi

Before practicing throwing techniques or engaging in randori, it is imperative to master *ukemi*, the technique of falling safely. There are four forms of ukemi: backward, to either side, forward and the forward roll.

34.

36.

37.

35.

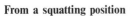

From a squatting position

34. Squat with your heels raised and your back straight.

35. Put your arms out in front of you.

36. Fall back, keeping your hips as close to your heels as possible.

37. Tuck in your chin and slap the mat with both hands and arms.

The main points to bear in mind when falling are to strike the mat hard with one or both arms, to curve the back, and to tuck in the chin so that your head does not hit the mat. Start from low positions and slow falls and gradually work up to falling from a standing position, then practice ukemi while moving or being thrown.

After you have mastered the forward fall from a kneeling position, practice from a squatting position and then from a standing position. Also practice falling to left and right front.

38.

40.

41.

42.

39.

43.

From a standing position

38. Stand naturally, with your feet close together.

39. Put your arms out in front of you.

40–42. Fall backward by lowering your hips.

43. Tuck in your chin, curve your back, and slap hard with both hands and arms, letting your legs go up in the air.

Falling Sideways

44.

45.

46.

47.

48.

49.

50.

From a sitting position

44–45. Sit upright with your legs stretched out. Bring your right arm across your chest, fingers extended, palm down.

46–47. Fall backward to your right back corner.

48. Tuck in your chin, curve your back, and slap the mat with your right hand and arm, letting your legs go up in the air.

49. Drop your legs and sit up.

50. Return to a sitting position. Repeat the above movements to your left.

51.   52.   53.

54.   55.   56.

From a squatting position

51. Squat with your hands on your upper thighs.

52–55. Bring your right arm across your chest. Advance your right leg to the left front corner.

56. Fall back to your right back corner.

57.

58.

59.

60.

61.

62.

From a standing position

57. Stand naturally, feet close together, arms at your sides.

58. Step to your left front corner with your left foot.

59–62. Advance your right foot in front of your left foot and fall back to your right back corner.

Falling Forward

63. 64. 65.

66. 67. 68.

69. 70. 71.

From a kneeling position

63. Kneel with your heels raised.

64. Let yourself fall forward. Just before your body hits the mat, slap down with both hands and forearms.

65. Your hands should be turned inward at a 45-degree angle so that your elbows bend outward. Your body is supported by your hands and toes. Do pushups to strengthen your arms for the forward fall.

From a squatting position

66. Squat with your hands on your thighs.

67. Fall forward. Just before hitting the mat, slap downward with both hands and forearms.

68. Your forearms should slant outward at a 45-degree angle. Support yourself on your hands and toes in position for doing pushups.

From a standing position

69. From a natural standing position with your feet close together and your arms at your sides, lean forward and let yourself fall.

70. Slap down with both hands and forearms just before your body hits the mat.

71. With your elbows slanted outward, you are again in position to do pushups.

Forward Roll

The forward fall will protect you in some situations, but if you fall from a height or are thrown forward with force, you must roll to avoid injury. Practice rolling from a crouching position first, then from a standing position. When you can roll smoothly without hurting your shoulder or flopping on your back, take a running start. Finally, practice jumping over obstacles. Alternate left and right rolls.

72.

73.

74.

75.

76.

77.

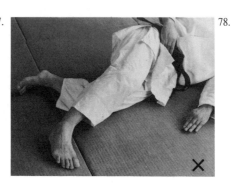
78.

From a crouching position

72. From the basic natural posture, step forward with your right foot, bend over, and put your left hand down (fingers turned inward) so that it forms a triangle with your feet. Then put your right hand down between your left hand and your right foot. Be sure that the fingers of your right hand point back through your legs, never toward the front.

73–75. Bend your right arm until it is rounded, tuck in your chin, and push off hard with your feet, rolling along your right arm, shoulder and back like a wheel.

76. As your legs come down, slap the mat with your left arm.

77. Do not let your legs cross. This is how they should look after the roll.

78. *Incorrect* position of the legs after the roll.

79.

80.

81.

82.

83.

84.

85.

86.

87.

From a standing position

79–84. From the basic natural posture, step forward with your right foot and roll as you did from a kneeling position.

85–87. After slapping the mat, use your forward momentum to return to a standing position.

UKEMI 53

The Running Roll

88. Start in the basic natural posture.

89–92. Run forward and kick off with your right foot. Put your rounded right arm down 60 to 90 centimeters in front of your right foot and roll on it. There is no need to use your left arm.

93. Slap the mat as your legs come down.

94. Continue the roll until you are on your feet again.

95. You should finish in a balanced posture, ready for anything.

5. Classification of Techniques

All judo techniques fall into one of three categories, and each category is further subdivided. The three categories are:

Nage-waza	Throwing Techniques
Katame-waza	Grappling Techniques
Atemi-waza	Striking Techniques

Nage-waza comprise *tachi-waza* (standing techniques) and *sutemi-waza* (sacrifice techniques).

The action of the hips is important in any *tachi-waza*, but they are further classified as either *te-waza* (hand techniques), *koshi-waza* (hip techniques) or *ashi-waza* (foot or leg techniques), depending on which part of the body plays the central role in executing the technique.

Sutemi-waza are called *ma-sutemi-waza* (supine sacrifice techniques) or *yoko-sutemi-waza* (side sacrifice techniques). The former involve taking a back-on-the-mat position, the latter a side-on-the-mat position.

Katame-waza comprise *osae-komi-waza* (hold-down techniques), *shime-waza* (strangling techniques) and *kansetsu-waza* (joint techniques). The term *ne-waza* (mat work) is sometimes used in place of *katame-waza*, but it is misleading in that not all *katame-waza* are executed while lying on the mat. Some strangleholds and joint locks, for example, can be applied from a standing position. As can be seen from the terminology, in grappling the opponent is held, his joints are locked or his limbs bent or twisted, or he can be strangled.

Atemi-waza are techniques for disabling an assailant by attacking with the fist, the knife edge of the hand, the fingertips, the elbow, the knee, the ball of the foot, the toes, the heel, the forehead or the back of the head. (*See* p. 137.) The technique may take the form of striking, punching, chopping, thrusting, jabbing or kicking. They are divided into *ude-waza* (arm strikes), in which vital points are attacked with the hand or arm, and *ashi-ate* (leg strikes), in which the leg or foot becomes a weapon. Both groups of techniques are further subdivided, as shown in the table below.

The result of making forceful contact with a vital point can be pain, loss of consciousness, coma, disablement or death. *Ate-waza* are practiced in kata, *never* in randori.

Nage-waza

Tachi-waza		
Te-waza	**Koshi-waza**	**Ashi-waza**
Tai-otoshi Seoi-nage Kata-guruma Uki-otoshi Sumi-otoshi Sukui-nage Obi-otoshi Seoi-otoshi Yama-arashi	Uki-goshi Harai-goshi Tsurikomi-goshi Hane-goshi O-goshi Ushiro-goshi Utsuri-goshi Tsuri-goshi Koshi-guruma	Hiza-guruma Kosoto-gari Ouchi-gari Kosoto-gake Osoto-gari Ashi-guruma Sasae-tsurikomi- Uchi-mata ashi O-guruma Harai-tsurikomi- Osoto-guruma ashi Osoto-otoshi Okuri-ashi-harai Deashi-harai Kouchi-gari

Sutemi-waza	
Ma-sutemi-waza	**Yoko-sutemi-waza**
Tomoe-nage Ura-nage Sumi-gaeshi Hikkomi-gaeshi Tawara-gaeshi	Uki-waza Yoko-otoshi Yoko-gake Hane-makikomi Yoko-guruma Soto-makikomi Tani-otoshi Uchi-makikomi Yoko-wakare

1. *Ouchi-gari.* Hitoshi Saito, 6th *dan.*

Katame-waza

Osae-komi-waza	Shime-waza	Kansetsu-waza
Hon-kesa-gatame	Nami-juji-jime	Ude-garami
Kuzure-kesa-gatame	Kata-juji-jime	Ude-hishigi-juji-gatame
Kata-gatame	Gyaku-juji-jime	Ude-hishigi-ude-gatame
Kami-shiho-gatame	Hadaka-jime	Ude-hishigi-hiza-gatame
Kuzure-kami-shiho-gatame	Okuri-eri-jime	Ude-hishigi-waki-gatame
Yoko-shiho-gatame	Kata-ha-jime	Ude-hishigi-hara-gatame
Tate-shiho-gatame	Katate-jime	Ude-hishigi-ashi-gatame
	Ryote-jime	Ude-hishigi-te-gatame
	Sode-guruma-jime	Ude-hishigi-sankaku-gatame
	Tsukkomi-jime	Ashi-garami
	Sankaku-jime	
	Do-jime	

2. *Kami-shiho-gatame.* Yasuhiro Yamashita, 7th *dan.*

3. *Yoko-shiho-gatame.* Yoshimi Masaki, 6th *dan.*

Atemi-waza

Ude-ate			
Yubisaki-ate	Kobushi-ate	Tegatana-ate	Hiji-ate
Ago-oshi Ryogan-tsuki Suri-age	Tsuki-kake (Tsukkake) Tsukiage (Kachi-kake) Yoko-uchi	Naname-uchi Kirioroshi Ushiro-dori	Ushiro-ate Ushiro-dori

Ashi-ate		
Hiza-gashira-ate	Sekito-ate	Kakato-ate
Ryote-dori Gyakute-dori	Keage Mae-geri Ryote-dori	Ushiro-geri Yoko-geri Ashi-fumi

6. Nage-waza

1. *Osoto-gari.* Yasuhiro Yamashita, 7th *dan.*

The first forty nage-waza introduced in this chapter constitute what is known as *Gokyo no Waza*, the five groups of instruction. Each group comprises eight representative techniques. Then come *Shimmeisho no Waza*, the new techniques developed after 1920. Learning the throws in order is the key to mastery. Once the main point of a technique has been thoroughly grasped, the acquired capability can be applied to variations.

In the following descriptions, techniques are executed from the right natural posture. They can, of course, and should be practiced from the left natural posture.

It is well to remember the traditional terms *tori* (taker) and *uke* (receiver), indicating, respectively, the person who throws and the person who is thrown. In these descriptions we have found it more suitable to use the second and third person pronouns, but *uke* and *tori* can often be heard in the dojo.

Gokyo no Waza: GROUP 1

Deashi-harai   **Forward Foot Sweep**

In this technique, you force your opponent to step forward, then sweep his advancing foot out from under him.

Timing is crucial in this and other throwing techniques. Your opponent must be just on the verge of placing his foot and most of his weight on the mat. (This timing is applicable to sweeping the back foot as well.) It is also important that you curve your left foot enough to catch his foot well below the ankle. (*Fig. 8*)

2.   3.   4.   5.

6.   7.

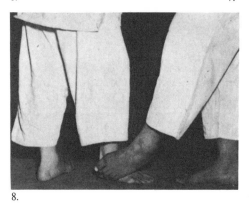

2. Begin in the right natural posture.

3. Step back a bit farther than usual with your right foot and pull your opponent forward with your whole body. He will take a large step with his left foot.

4. Loosen your right grip a bit and pull him toward you with your left hand so that he brings his right foot up close to his left.

5. Just as he is putting his right foot down, sweep it in the direction it is traveling with your left foot.

6. As you sweep, pull down hard with your left hand.

7. Your opponent will fall, slapping the mat with his left hand and arm.

8.

Hiza-guruma   Knee Wheel

After breaking your opponent's balance to his right front corner, place your left foot on his right kneecap and throw him over it.

Pay particular attention to the placement of your right foot. It should be neither too close to nor too far from your opponent. Be sure to curl the toes of your left foot inward and to put it just on the side of his right kneecap. (*Figs. 16–17*) To throw an opponent to his left from a right posture, change your right grip from his left lapel to the left middle outer sleeve. (*Fig. 18*)

Beginners may find it easier to step back with their left foot and execute the throw when the opponent steps forward with his right foot into the right defensive posture.

9.

10.

11.

12.

16.

17.

18.

13.

14.

15.

9. Begin in the right natural posture.

10. Step forward with your left foot to make your opponent step back with his right foot.

11. Lightly draw him to his right front corner by pulling and lifting with both hands.

12–14. As your opponent loses his balance, place the sole of your left foot against the side of his right kneecap. At the same time, twist your body to the left and pull hard with both hands in a sharp downward curve. Your opponent's body will pivot over your left foot.

15. As he hits the mat, pull up on his right sleeve to break his fall.

Sasae-tsurikomi-ashi   Supporting Foot Lift-Pull Throw

You break your opponent's balance to his right front corner and throw him by blocking his right leg with your left foot. Your sole should be placed just above his ankle. (*Fig. 29*)

Be sure to lean backward and twist to the left as you throw. Neither blocking nor pulling will be effective if you bend forward at the waist.

19.

20.

21.

22.

23.

24.

25.

26.

27.

28.

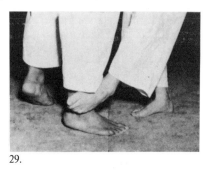
29.

19. Begin in the right natural posture.

20. Step forward with your left foot and push your opponent with both hands so that he steps back with his right foot.

21. Step back with your left foot while pulling and lifting to his right front corner.

22. Your opponent will come forward with his right foot in an effort to regain his balance.

23–24. Before he can bring it forward, place the sole of your left foot against his right shin.

25–28. At the same time, twist back toward your left, pulling hard with your left hand and pushing with your right.

Uki-goshi   Floating Hip Throw

After breaking your opponent's balance to his right front corner, you load him on your hip and throw him by twisting your hip to the left. Wrap your arm as far as possible around his body. (*Fig. 33*)

The throw differs from *o-goshi* in that you do not raise your hips or bend forward.

30.

31.

33.   32.

30. Begin in the right natural posture. While turning to the right, pull your opponent with your right hand to make him step forward with his left foot. Break his balance to his right front corner by pulling a bit with your left hand. Put your right arm around his waist and step in close to him, placing your right foot parallel to his in front of his instep. Bring your left foot back and hold him firmly against your hip.

31. Twist your hips.

32. Pull up on his left sleeve as he falls.

Osoto-gari   **Large Outer Reap**

You break your opponent's balance toward his right back corner, causing him to shift all his weight toward his right heel, and reap his right leg with your right leg.

You should step as far left of his right foot as you can so that you can put power into the reaping action. (*Fig. 41*)

34.

35.

36.

37.

38.

39.

40.

41.

34. Begin in the right natural posture.

35. Make your opponent step forward with his right foot by pulling him gently to his right front corner. Put your left foot outside his right foot to break his balance to his right back corner by pulling him toward you with your left hand and pushing him backward with your right.

36. Lightly raise your right leg and swing it past your opponent's right leg.

37. Clip his thigh hard from behind with your thigh.

38–39. At the same time, pull down hard with your left hand and push toward his right back corner with your right hand.

40. Your opponent's legs will fly up and he will fall directly backward.

O-goshi   Large Hip Throw

To execute *o-goshi*, you break your opponent's balance directly forward or to his right front corner, load him onto your right hip, then raise your hip and twist to throw him.

This throw differs from uki-goshi in that you insert your hip low and raise it as you throw.

From the right natural posture it is difficult to put your right arm around your opponent, since he has hold of your right sleeve. Let go of his left lapel and pass your right hand under and up over his left arm at the elbow and then under his armpit. This causes his elbow to lock and he will release his grip, at which point you can put your right arm around his waist. (*Fig. 49*)

42.   43.   44.   45.

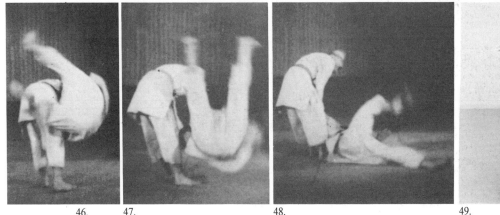

46. 47.   48.   49.

42. Begin in the right defensive posture. Pull your opponent toward you with your right hand so that he steps forward with his left foot.

43. Quickly slip your right arm around his waist and draw him toward your right hip, breaking his balance to the front.

44. Pivot around, placing your right foot in front of his right instep, parallel to his foot, and your left foot slightly in front of his left foot.

45. Bend your knees and pull him tight against your right hip. Lift him up by straightening your knees.

46. At the same time, pull with your left arm and twist to the left.

47–48. Your opponent will turn over your hip and fall on his back in front of you.

Ouchi-gari   ## Large Inner Reap

After breaking your opponent's balance to his left back corner, reap his left leg from the inside with your right leg so that he falls backward.

Be sure to twist your hips to the left as you attack so that you can insert your right leg heel first, toes pointed in, and reap widely to the right. (*Fig. 57*)

50.   51.   52.   53.

54.   55.   56.

57.

50–51. Begin in the right natural posture. Take a small step forward with your left foot, raise and draw back your right foot a little, and pull your opponent toward his left front corner with your right hand.

52. He will advance his left foot.

53–54. Just before he sets his foot down, slip your right leg in behind his left leg, bringing the back of your knee against the back of his left knee.

55. Clip the leg in a wide arc toward your right back corner.

56. Push your opponent directly downward with both hands.

Seoi-nage   **Shoulder Throw**

You break your opponent's balance straight to the front or to his right front corner, load him on your back, and throw him over your shoulder.

As you pull your opponent onto your back with your left arm, your right arm will naturally bend. Your opponent's right arm should cover your elbow.

A variation of this technique is called *ippon-seoi-nage* (one-arm shoulder throw). Your left hand holds your opponent's right inner sleeve. As you pivot, slip your right arm through his right armpit and grab the top of his sleeve or his right shoulder. In other respects, execution of the technique is the same. (*Fig. 67*)

58.   59.   60.   61.   62.

63.   64.   65.   66.   67.

58. Begin in the right natural posture.

59. Step forward with your left foot and push with both hands to make your opponent step back with his right foot.

60. Now step forward with your right foot and push so that he steps back with his left foot.

61. The purpose of pushing is to make your opponent push back. When he does, and begins to come forward with his left foot, step back with your right foot more than he has pushed so as to pull him off balance to his front.

62. Pivot to the left and put your right foot in front of his right instep, parallel to his foot.

63. Lower your body by bending your knees, and place your left foot in front of his left instep. Bend your right elbow.and put it under your opponent's right armpit.

64. Pull him close to you and straighten your legs.

65. Now bend your body forward and pull downward with both hands.

66. Your opponent will fly over your right shoulder and land in front of you.

Gokyo no Waza: GROUP 2

Kosoto-gari   Small Outer Reap

You first break your opponent's balance to his right back corner, then reap his right foot from behind with your left foot and throw him backward.

Be sure to place your right foot at a right angle to your opponent's right foot. (*Fig. 75*) Ideally the sole of your left foot skims the mat as you reap and your big toe is raised, but it is permissible to twist your foot and reap with the sole.

68.   69.   70.   71.

72.   73.   74.   75.

68. While in the right natural posture, pull your opponent lightly to his front with both hands. To keep his balance, he pulls back.

69. Break his balance to his right back corner with both hands so that his weight is on his heels.

70. Step to his right side with your left foot, then your right, so that you stand at a right angle to him.

71. Clip his right foot in the direction of his toes, catching it just above the heel with your left foot.

72-73. At the same time, pull down with your left hand and push up and back with your right.

74. Your opponent should fall on his back at your feet.

Kouchi-gari   ## Small Inner Reap

After breaking your opponent's balance to his right back corner, you reap his right foot from the inside with your right foot and throw him backward.

Timing is crucial. Reap the foot just as he is placing his weight on it. As with kosoto-gari, ideally you skim the mat with the sole of your right foot, and reap with your big toe raised. In any case, push your opponent's foot forward, not upward, with the little-toe side of your foot brushing the mat. (*Fig. 83*)

76.　77.　　　　　　78.　　　　　　79.　　　　　80.

81.　　　　82.

83.

76. While standing in the right natural posture, lightly push your opponent to his left back corner.

77. When he pushes back, pull him with your left arm while bringing your left foot behind your right.

78. Pull with your body to make him advance his right foot.

79. Just before he puts his foot down, shift your weight to your left foot and clip his right heel from the inside with your right foot.

80. Keep his foot going in the direction his toes are pointing.

81. At the same time, push backward and downward with both hands.

82. When the throw is done well, your opponent's legs will fly up in the air on either side of you.

Koshi-guruma   **Hip Wheel**

While breaking your opponent's balance to his front or to his right front corner, you put your right hip solidly against his and throw him over it.

Your left hand must pull strongly and continuously. At least half your right hip should project beyond your opponent's right side. (*Fig. 92*)

84.   85.   86.   87.   88.

89.   90.   91.   92.

84. From the right natural posture, step back with your right foot to cause your opponent to bring his left foot forward.

85. Pull gently with both hands until his weight is on his toes.

86. Put your right foot near his right foot and slip your right arm around his neck or shoulder.

87. Continue pivoting, bringing your left foot back until your right hip is against the left of his abdomen. Thrust your right hip in deeply.

88–90. While raising your hips and pulling to the front with both hands, twist toward your left front.

91. Your opponent will fall over your hip and land in front of you.

Tsurikomi-goshi   Lift-Pull Hip Throw

When your opponent's balance has been broken to his front or to his right front corner, you drop your hips to the level of his thighs, then by raising your hips and pulling with both hands, throw him over your hips.

A variant of this throw is called *sode-tsurikomi-goshi* (sleeve lift-pull hip throw). It differs from the standard throw in that your right hand holds your opponent's left outer sleeve or cuff instead of his lapel. (*Figs. 101-2*)

93.   94.   95.   96.   97.

98.   99.   100.   101.   102.

93. From the right natural posture, step back with your right foot. As your opponent comes forward with his left foot, pull him off balance to his front.

94. Break his balance to his right front corner by lifting and pulling with both hands. At the same time, put your right foot between his feet.

95. Slip your right elbow underneath his left armpit and turn to your left. Your feet should be pointing in the same direction as his.

96. Drop your hips and bring them against his right front thigh.

97. As you load him onto your right hip, straighten your legs and push your hips backward.

98. Pull down hard with both hands.

99–100. Your opponent will turn over your hips and fall on his back in front of you.

Okuri-ashi-harai   **Foot Sweep**

You break your opponent's balance to his right side and sweep his right foot toward his left with your left foot.

For the technique to work, you must stay loose and move smoothly. Put the sole of your foot as close as possible to his outer ankle and sweep just as he is shifting his weight to his left foot. (*Fig. 111*) Be sure to sweep with your whole leg, not just your foot. Sweep in the direction his foot is traveling.

103. Begin in the right natural posture.

104. Your opponent steps to his left back corner. Take a step to your right front corner.

105. As he moves his right foot to the left, pursue it with your left.

106. Just before he puts his weight on it, sweep it with the sole of your left foot in the direction it is moving.

107. At the same time, lift up with your right hand and push down with your left.

108–110. Your opponent's legs will fly out from under him and he will land on his back.

Tai-otoshi   Body Drop

Having broken your opponent's balance to his right front corner or to his right side, you place your right foot past his right foot and throw him over your foot to your right front corner with the action of both hands.

Be careful not to put your right foot too far past your opponent's foot. (*Fig. 119*) Your right hand should push in the direction your opponent is falling, not pull.

112.   113.   114.   115.

116.   117.   118.

119.

112. Begin in the right natural posture.

113. Take a small step back with your right foot and pull your opponent forward, then break his balance to his right front corner by pulling and lifting.

114. Quickly step back wide with your left foot and place your right foot slightly past his right foot.

115. Pull forward and downward with your left hand while pushing with your right in the direction he is moving.

116–18. Your opponent will fall over your foot in a big circle and land to your right front.

Harai-goshi   **Hip Sweep**

You break your opponent's balance to his right front corner, pivot and pull him to you, then sweep his right thigh with your right thigh.

The technique was devised as a means of throwing an opponent who slips past your hip when you attempt uki-goshi.

120.
121.
122.
123.
124.
125.

120. Begin in the right natural posture.

121. Step back with your left foot and break your opponent's balance by pulling and lifting with both hands. Swing your left foot around and place it in front of his left foot.

122. At the same time, continue pulling with both hands until his chest and abdomen come into contact with your torso.

123. Stick your right leg past his right leg and sweep upward and outward against his thigh with the back of your thigh.

124. Twist to the left and pull strongly forward and downward with both hands.

125–26. Your opponent will land on his back in front of you.

126.

Uchi-mata   Inner-thigh Reaping Throw

After breaking your opponent's balance to his front or to his right front corner, you sweep his left inner thigh from within with the back of your right thigh. Execute the throw just as your opponent's weight is shifting to his left foot.

In the variation where you slide your left leg between your opponent's legs, your left foot should point in the same direction as his right foot. (*Fig. 136*)

127.   128.   129.   130.   131.

132.   133.   134.   135.

136.

127. Begin in the right natural posture, with your right hand held a little higher than usual.

128. Pull with your right hand, and when your opponent begins to step forward with his left foot, move your left foot to your left front corner and step back a bit with your right.

129. Pull him in a large circle toward your right back corner with your right hand.

130. He will move his left foot toward his left front corner and bend over.

131. Just before he places his left foot on the mat, step in a little with your left foot.

132. Sweep your right thigh up against his left inner thigh.

133. Pull to your left with your left hand and push in that direction with your right.

134-35. The upward sweep of your thigh lifts your opponent up, while the action of your hands causes him to roll over and land on his back.

Gokyo no Waza: GROUP 3

Kosoto-gake   **Small Outer Hook**

You break your opponent's balance to his right back corner, hook his right ankle with your left foot, and throw him backward.

The movement of your hands must be smooth, continuous and coordinated with your hip and foot movements. If you bend your left leg a little before placing your foot on your opponent's ankle, you can put more power into the throw. (*Fig. 146*)

This technique developed as a variation of kosoto-gari, but it is now considered an independent technique.

137.   138.   139.   140.

141.   142.   143.   144.

146.

145.

137. Begin in the right natural posture.

138. Step back with your right foot and pull your opponent with your hands.

139. He should come forward with his left foot, then take a large step with his right.

140. Break his balance to his right back corner by pushing upward toward your left front corner with your right hand, which is holding his left lapel, and push backward and downward with your left.

141. Place the ball of your left foot on his right outer ankle and heel.

142. Hook or reap it as if to lift him up.

143. Continue pushing down and back with your hands.

144–45. Your opponent will fall toward his right back corner.

Tsuri-goshi   **Lifting Hip Throw**

After breaking your opponent's balance to the front, you grab his belt at the back with your right hand, pull him onto your hip, and throw him forward by twisting.

There are two forms of tsuri-goshi, known as *kotsuri-goshi* (small hip throw) and *otsuri-goshi* (large hip throw). In the former, better suited to a small person, the right hand is passed through the opponent's left armpit, while in the latter, better suited to a large person, the right arm goes over the opponent's left arm. (*Fig. 156*) Kotsuri-goshi is illustrated here.

147.   148.   149.   150.

151.   152.   153.   154.

155.

156.

147. While in the right natural posture, take a half-step back with your right foot so that your opponent comes forward with his left.

148. While breaking his balance to the front, put your right hand through his left armpit and grab his belt at the back.

149. Turn and put your right foot at the inside front of his right foot, parallel to it, and bring your left foot outside his.

150. Bend your knees and pull him tightly against you by lifting with both hands.

151. Raise him on your hips.

152. While lifting his body with your right hand, straighten your knees and twist your hips.

153. At the same time, pull down hard with your left hand.

154–55. Your opponent falls at your feet.

Yoko-otoshi   **Side Drop**

Breaking your opponent's balance to his right side, you place your left foot outside his right foot and throw him to your left by dropping to your left side. This is a technique that can be practiced without a partner. (*Fig. 163*)

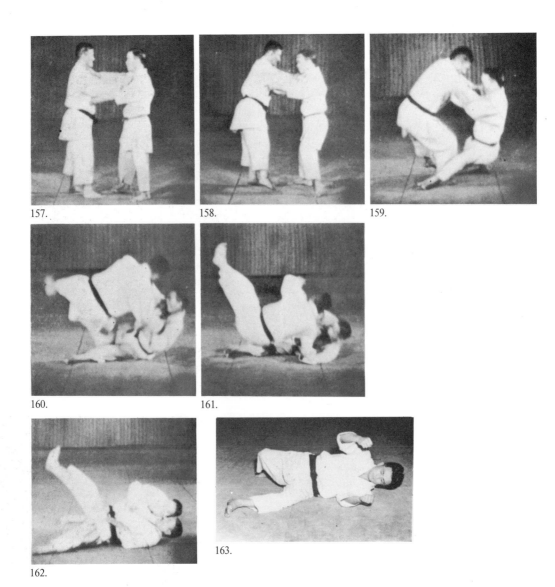

157.   158.   159.

160.   161.

163.

162.

157. Begin in the right natural posture.

158. Step to your right and try to break your opponent's balance to his left.

159. He resists by shifting his weight to his right. Break his balance to his right.

160. Place your left foot at the outside of his right ankle and drop to your left.

161. As you fall, pull to your left with both hands.

162. Your opponent will land almost parallel to you.

Ashi-guruma   **Leg Wheel**

Having broken your opponent's balance to his right front corner, you pivot and extend your right leg across his right knee and throw him over your leg in a large circle.

In the placement of the leg above the opponent's knee, the throw resembles hiza-guruma. (*Fig. 172*)

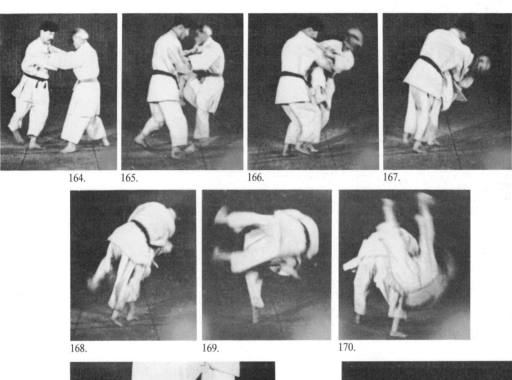

164.   165.   166.   167.

168.   169.   170.

172.

164–65. From the right natural posture, step back with your right foot and pull to bring your opponent forward on his left foot, then his right. Break his balance to his right front corner with your hands.

166. Bring your left foot around behind you and pivot to the left. Stick your right leg across your opponent's legs and press it against his right knee-cap, your ankle extending slightly past it.

167. Draw him close to you with both hands and twist to the left.

168–71. His body will rotate over your leg.

171.

Hane-goshi   **Hip Spring**

You break your opponent's balance to his right front corner, pull him to your right hip, and throw him with an upward springing action of your right hip and leg combined with a downward pull by both hands.

For the technique to work properly, the movements of your hips, legs and hands must be well coordinated. Be sure your right knee projects past your opponent's right leg so that your leg, hip and chest make full contact with the front of his body.

173.

174.

175.

176.

177.

178.

179.

180.

173. While in the right natural posture, break your opponent's balance to his right front corner.

174. Bring your left foot around behind you.

175. At the same time, bend your right knee and place the leg against the inside of his right leg.

176. With both hands, pull him to you and load him onto your hip.

177. Straighten your left leg and lift him off the mat with the springing action of your right hip and leg.

178. Twist to the left and pull out and down hard with both hands.

179–80. Your opponent should turn over your right hip and land at your feet.

Harai-tsurikomi-ashi   ## Lift-Pull Foot Sweep

After breaking your opponent's balance to his left front corner, you sweep his left ankle with your right foot and throw him to his left. To avoid sweeping too high, brush his left instep with the little-toe side of your right foot. (*Fig. 189*)

A simpler way to do harai-tsurikomi-ashi from the right natural posture is to step forward with your left foot, quickly bring your right up near it, and sweep your opponent's right foot as he draws it back. Beginners may want to practice the simpler version first.

181.

184.

187.

182.

185.

188.

183.

186.

189.

181. From the right natural posture, step forward with your left foot to make your opponent step back with his right.

182. Break his balance to his left front corner by lifting and pulling (*tsurikomi*).

183. Move your left foot close to his right.

184. Stretch your right leg out, and with the sole of your foot sweep his left outer ankle or shin away

from you.

185. At the same time, twist your upper body to your right and pull hard toward your right armpit with your right hand, which is holding his left lapel.

186. Push upward and toward your right with your left hand.

187–88. Your opponent should fall in a large circle to his left.

Tomoe-nage   **Circular Throw**

Here you bring your opponent onto his toes, drop backward while placing your right foot on his lower abdomen, and throw him back over your head.

It is important that your left sole be firmly on the mat when you slide it between your opponent's legs. Your right knee should be bent and your toes pulled back when you place your foot on your opponent's abdomen. The throw is accomplished by the joint action of your hands and your right leg, so it is necessary to keep up a constant pull, first forward, then downward. (*Fig. 198*)

190.

191.

192.

193.

194.

195.

196.

197.

198.

190. Begin in the right natural posture.

191. Step forward with your left foot and push your opponent hard directly backward. He pushes back and comes forward with his right foot. Move your left hand to his right lapel.

192. While pulling him onto his toes with both hands, slip your left foot in between his legs, bend your left knee and sit back, placing your hips as close to your left heel as possible.

193. At the same time, bend your right knee and lightly put the sole of your right foot on his lower abdomen.

194. Push his body up by straightening your right leg, and pull with both hands.

195-97. Your opponent will fly over your head and land on the mat some distance from you.

Kata-guruma   **Shoulder Wheel**

While breaking your opponent's balance to his right front corner, you lift him onto your shoulders and drop him on the mat. Step in as deeply as possible with your right foot. The back of your head should be at the right side of his belt. (*Fig. 208*)

199.   200.   201.   202.

203.   204.   205.

206.   207.   208.

199. From the right natural posture, move your left foot back and pull your opponent forward with both hands.

200. As he comes further forward with his right foot, take his right middle inner sleeve with your left hand and break his balance to his right front corner.

201. Bend your knees and step in under him with your right foot.

202. As you do so, put your right arm around his right thigh and load him onto your right shoulder.

203. Pull your left hand down toward your chest and straighten up.

204. Your opponent's weight is evenly distributed on your shoulders.

205-7. Throw him down to your left front.

Sumi-gaeshi   **Corner Throw**

After breaking your opponent's balance to his right front corner, you fall back, place the instep of your right foot in the crook of his left knee or on his thigh, and throw him up and over your head.

Power in this technique can be augmented by raising your right leg while you are falling, rather than after your back hits the mat. (*Fig. 216*)

209.

210.

211.

212.

213.

214.

215.

216.

209. Begin in the right defensive posture, with your and your opponent's right arms passing through each other's left armpits. Your right hand should be as high up on the top left corner of his back as possible. Hold his right arm tightly against you.

210. Pull him to his left front corner so that he steps forward with his left foot, then his right.

211. Just as he is coming forward with his right foot, move your left foot forward and break his balance to his right front corner. Drop onto your back directly beneath him.

212. At the same time, place the instep of your right foot in the crook of his left knee or on his inner thigh, and lift him up over you.

213. Pull with your left hand and push with your right.

214–15. Your opponent should roll from his right shoulder onto his back.

Tani-otoshi   **Valley Drop**

You break your opponent's balance to his right back corner, slide your left foot past the outside of his right foot, and throw him to his right back corner.

Tani-otoshi differs from yoko-otoshi in that you throw to your opponent's back corners rather than to one side. (*Figs. 223–26*)

217.   218.   219.   220.

221.   222.

223.   224.   225.   226.

217. From the right natural posture you try to break your opponent's balance to his right front corner. He pulls his right leg back.

218. Advance your left foot and break his balance to his right back corner.

219. Slide your left foot outside his right foot.

220. Lift and push with your right hand under his armpit. Pull with your left hand and turn your upper body to the left. Fall to your left front corner.

221–22. With his right leg blocked, your opponent falls to his right back corner.

Note: In the basic form of this technique, the opponent is thrown directly to the rear.

Hane-makikomi   **Springing Wraparound Throw**

This technique is a combination of hane-goshi and *soto-makikomi.* You break your opponent's balance to his right front corner, and while executing hane-goshi, wrap his body around yours and fall to the mat.

It is usual in going from hane-goshi to makikomi to release the hold of your right hand and pin your opponent's right arm in your right armpit. (*Fig. 233*)

227.   228.   229.

230.   231.   232.

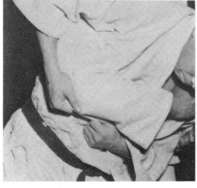

227. While in the right natural posture, break your opponent's balance to his right front corner by lifting and pulling with both hands.

228. Bring your left foot around behind you, bend your right leg, and pull him against the side of your body.

229. Let go with your right hand but continue pulling with your left.

230. Twist to the left and fall on your right side.

231–32. Your opponent, who is wrapped around you, falls with you.

233.

Sukui-nage   **Scooping Throw**

Having broken your opponent's balance to his left front corner, you pick him up in your arms and drop him to your right rear.

A good time to apply this throw in competition is when you are coming forward to grab your opponent after having separated from him. To prevent him from blocking the throw, it must be executed on your own initiative, before your opponent has a chance to grab you.

234.   235.   236.   237.

238.   239.   240.   241.

234. You are in the right natural posture and your opponent steps forward with his right foot, then his left.

235. Break his balance to his left back corner.

236. Step behind him with your right foot.

237. Reach your right hand around his waist from the front and take his left leg from behind with your left hand.

238. Lift him onto the front of your right hip.

239–41. Without looking back, drop him to your rear.

Utsuri-goshi   # Hip Shift

This throw is a *go no sen no waza*—a counter throw. It is used to counter an opponent's hip technique. After blocking his throw by bending your knees, you swing him onto your own hip and throw him by twisting your hips as in o-goshi.

To swing him up high, change your right-hand grip to his left middle inner sleeve. The throw can also be executed by simply stepping in front of your opponent with your left foot and loading him onto your left hip.

242. 243. 244.

245. 246.

247. 248.

242. Begin in the right natural posture.

243. Your opponent attempts a right hane-goshi. As he moves in, lower your hips, grab his rear belt with your left hand, and lift him with your arms and waist.

244. Swing him to your left and twist your hips to the right.

245. Continue swinging him up to your left and put your left hip under him, letting your left foot come slightly forward.

246-48. Shift your right-hand grip to his left sleeve and pull down hard with your right hand as you continue twisting your hips to the right.

O-guruma   Large Wheel

You break your opponent's balance to his right front corner, place your right leg across his lower abdomen, and throw him over it.

The throw differs from harai-goshi in that it depends mainly on the action of the legs rather than the movement of the hips. (*Fig. 256*)

249. 250.   251.   252.

253.   254.   255.

256.

249. Begin in the right natural posture.

250. Move your left foot forward while breaking your opponent's balance to his right front corner.

251. Turn to your left and stretch your right leg out straight across his upper legs.

252. Lift him by swinging your right leg up and back.

253. At the same time, pull down with both hands.

254–55. Your opponent's body should turn over your leg.

Soto-makikomi   **Outer Wraparound Throw**

While breaking your opponent's balance to his right front corner, you pull him close to you, twist to your left in a circle so that his body wraps around yours, and fall forward, sending him over your back.

In wrapping your opponent around you, grip his right outer sleeve at the elbow with your right hand and his right lower outer sleeve with your left hand. Keep his right arm firmly under your right arm. (*Fig. 263*)

257.

258.

259.

260.

261.

262.

263.

257. While in the right natural posture, break your opponent's balance to his right front corner.

258. To retain his balance, he steps forward with his right foot, then his left.

259. When he is about to shift his weight to his right foot, turn to your left and bring your left foot back around you.

260. Put your right foot to the outside of his right foot and release your right grip.

261. Pull him to your right side with your left hand.

262. Continue twisting to the left, wrapping his body around yours, and throw yourself forward and downward.

Uki-otoshi   **Floating Drop**

You break your opponent's balance to his right front corner and pull him downward with both hands, causing him to fall forward in a circle.

Another way to do the technique is to step back and drop to your left knee, left toes raised. Pull hard using the combined power of both arms. (*Fig. 271*) This form of the throw is done in the throwing kata and is often the more effective of the two.

264.   265.   266.

267.   268.   269.

270.

271.

264. From the right natural posture, step forward with your left foot so that your opponent steps back with his right foot.

265. Take a large step back with your left foot. As he comes forward with his right foot, break his balance to his right front corner.

266. Just as his weight is coming onto his right foot, twist your upper body to the left.

267. Pull down with your left hand while pushing up with your right, which is holding his left lapel.

268–70. Your opponent should fall in a circle to his right front corner.

Gokyo no Waza: GROUP 5

Osoto-guruma   **Large Outer Wheel**

After breaking your opponent's balance to his right back corner or straight back, you put your right leg across the back of his right knee and throw him back over it. Your right thigh acts as the fulcrum.

An alternative way to execute this throw using the same hand action is to break the opponent's balance to his right front corner or directly forward, then place your left knee against his left thigh and throw. (*Fig. 279*)

272.

273.

274.

275.

276.

277.

278.

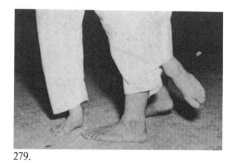
279.

272. Begin in the right natural posture.

273. Pull your opponent up and push him (*tsuri-komi*) to his right back corner or rear, then bring your left foot alongside his right.

274. Feint a leg reap with your right leg. Your opponent resists by leaning forward.

275. Stretch your right leg across the back of both his legs from his right thigh to his left knee.

276. Push hard with your right hand and pull close to your side with your left.

277-78. Unable to step back to regain his balance, your opponent falls back over your leg.

Uki-waza   **Floating Throw**

Having broken your opponent's balance to his right front corner, you block his right foot with your left foot and throw him over you by falling on your left side.

For the technique to be successful, excellent coordination is necessary when sacrificing your standing posture to make full use of the power available. It is not absolutely necessary to step back with your right foot before extending your left foot well out to the side.

280.

281.

282.

283.

284.

285.

286.

280. From the right natural posture, step back with your right foot and when your opponent comes forward with his left, break his balance to his left front corner.

281. To recover his balance, he will bring his right foot forward.

282. Just at that moment, slide your left foot out-side his right foot.

283. Drop back to your left.

284. While falling, pull your left hand in an arc toward your body and push your right in an arc to the left.

285–86. Your opponent falls forward to his right front corner.

Yoko-wakare   **Side Separation**

You break your opponent's balance to his front and sacrifice yourself by dropping on your back and left side. Throw him across your outstretched body.

This technique is used mainly to counter uki-goshi, o-goshi and seoi-nage. Stepping quickly around your opponent's hip, you take advantage of his forward motion to throw him. (*Figs. 295–98*).

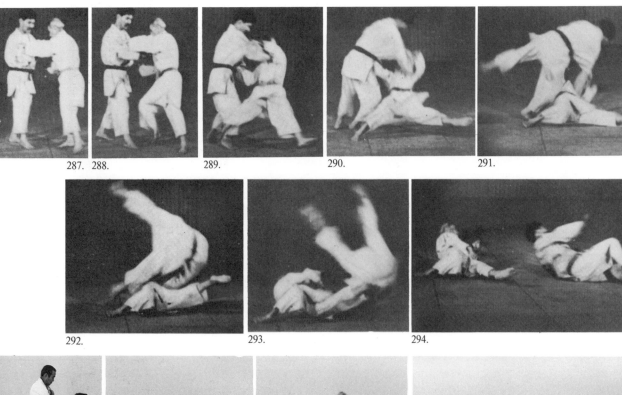

287. 288.   289.   290.   291.

292.   293.   294.

295. 296.   297.   298.

287. Begin in the right natural posture.

288. Pull your opponent a bit to bring him forward more on his left foot, then break his balance forward and step outside his left foot with your left foot.

289. Bring your right foot forward, too, slide your left foot out to the left, and drop on your left side.

290. Pull down hard with both hands as you fall.

291–94. Your opponent falls forward over your body and lands at a right angle to you.

Note: In the basic form of this technique, the opponent is thrown to his right (or left) front corner.

Yoko-guruma   # Side Wheel

This technique can be used to throw a person who bends forward in an effort to keep you from throwing him to the rear with utsuri-goshi or some similar technique. Slipping your right leg in between his legs, you drop on your right side and throw him back over your head.

299.   300.   301.

302.   303.

304.   305.   306.

299. Begin in the right natural posture.

300. Your opponent has tried to throw you with hange-goshi or o-goshi and you put your arms around him to counter with ura-nage or utsuri-goshi.

301. He reacts by bending forward.

302. Insert your right leg deep between his legs.

303. Drop on your right side while pulling him to you with your left hand and pushing up with your right.

304–6. Your opponent flies over your head and lands just past your left shoulder.

Ushiro-goshi   ## Back Hip Throw

Ushiro-goshi is used to counter a hip throw. Putting your arms around your opponent's waist from behind, you lean backward, swing him up in the air, and drop him on his back.

This must be done quickly or your opponent may wrap his legs around yours. The left knee as well as the arms may be used to swing him off the mat.

307.   308.   309.

310.   311.   312.

313.   314.

307. Begin in the right natural posture.

308. Your opponent attempts a hip throw.

309. Lower your hips and put both arms around his waist.

310. While holding him close to you, straighten your legs and bend your body backward.

311. Swing him up off the mat.

312. As he begins to come down, move your legs back.

313–14. Bend forward and pull him down to the mat so that he cannot land on his feet.

Ura-nage   **Back Throw**

You put both arms around your opponent from his right side (or from behind, *Fig. 323*), lift him up, and throw him back over your left shoulder as you sacrifice yourself by falling backward.

Be careful not to throw your opponent on his head.

315. 316.   317.   318.

319.   320.   321.

322.   323.

315. Begin in the right natural posture.

316. Your opponent attempts to throw you with a right hip technique. Step close so him with your left foot and lower your hips.

317. Put your arms around him from his right side.

318. Straighten your legs and bend backward to raise him.

319. Throw him back as you fall directly to your rear.

320–22. Your opponent goes flying over your left shoulder.

Sumi-otoshi   **Corner Drop**

After breaking your opponent's balance to his right back corner, you throw him in that direction with your hands.

This is an especially difficult technique, since it depends almost entirely on the hands. It will not work unless done very skillfully and with perfect timing. Note especially how your upper body is twisted somewhat to the right as you push your opponent.

The only difference between sumi-otoshi and uki-otoshi is the direction in which you throw. The principle involved is quite the same.

324. Begin in the right natural posture.

325. Step back with your right foot and draw your opponent forward on his left.

326. Lower your hips and step outside his right foot with your left.

327. At the same time, push him hard toward his right back corner with your right hand and pull with your left.

328. His left leg should fly up in the air.

329–31. Continuing to push with your right hand, pull with your left and he will flip over on his back.

Yoko-gake   **Side Body Drop**

After shifting your opponent's balance to his right front corner, break it straight to his right. Sweep his right leg out from under him, and throw him to his right by falling onto your left side.

Your hands, foot sweep and sacrifice must work together. Your sweep should be smooth and strong, not merely a kick.

332.   333.   334.   335.

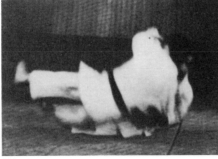 

336.   337.

338.   339.

332. From the right natural posture, step back with your right foot and draw your opponent forward on his left.

333. Then step back a bit with your left and draw him forward on his right. Break his balance to his right front corner.

334. Break his balance to his right by pushing him lightly to his right with your right hand and pulling

with your left.

335. Drop toward your left.

336. At the same time, sweep his right outer ankle toward his left leg with the sole of your left foot.

337-38. Keep up a strong downward pull with your left hand.

339. Your opponent will land almost parallel to you.

Shimmeisho no Waza

The Gokyo no Waza were formally set forth in 1895 and revised in 1920. Since then, a number of new techniques have come into widespread use. After careful consideration, the Kodokan has decided to include the following seventeen within the body of officially recognized throwing techniques.

Morote-gari

340. 341. 342. 343.

Kuchiki-taoshi

346. Step in between your opponent's legs with your right foot.

347. Quickly grab his right leg, either from the inside with your right hand or from the outside with your left.

348–51. Lift the leg up and push him backward and down.

346. 347.

Kibisu-gaeshi

352. 353. 354. 355.

Hand Techniques

Two-Hand Reap

344.

345.

340. Step in between your opponent's legs with your right foot.

341. Throw your shoulders into his chest, and put your arms around his legs, just above the knees.

342–45. Reap his legs toward you and throw him directly to his rear.

One-Hand Drop

348.

349.

350.

351.

Heel Trip

356.

357.

352. Step outside your opponent's right foot with your left.

353. Drop your hips.

354–57. Reap his right foot from behind with your right or left hand as in kouchi-gari or kosoto-gari.

Uchi-mata-sukashi   Inner Thigh Reaping Throw Slip

358.

359.

360.

361.

362.

363.

358–63. As your opponent moves in for a right uchi-mata, slip past his reaping leg and use his momentum to throw him forward.

Hip Techniques

Dakiage   High Lift

364.

365.

366.

367.

364. When your opponent is on his back on the mat, move in between his legs.

365. Slip your hands under his legs and grab his belt on either side.

366–67. Raise your right knee, draw him to you and stand.

Note: This technique is not permitted in randori or tournaments.

Foot and Leg Techniques

Tsubame-gaeshi   Swallow Counter

368.   369.   370.   371.   372.

368. Your opponent attempts a right deashi-harai.
369. Shift your weight to your left leg and withdraw your right foot by bending your knee.
370-74. Throw him with a left deashi-harai.

373.   374.

Osoto-gaeshi   Large Outer Reaping Throw Counter

375.   376.   377.   378.   380.

379.

375-77. Your opponent moves in for a right osoto-gari.
378-80. Before he has a chance to get you off balance to your right rear, apply your own right osoto-gari.

381.   382.   383.   384.

385.   386.   387.   388.

389.   390.   391.   392.

381. Your opponent attacks with a right ouchi-gari.

382–84. When he has hooked your left leg with his right, sweep the leg out and throw him to his right rear.

385. Alternatively, raise your left leg before your opponent can hook it.

386–88. Throw him with your arms to his right rear.

389–92. Another possibility after raising your left leg is to throw him to his left front corner.

406.   407.

Kouchi-gaeshi   Small Inner Reaping Throw Counter

393.

394.

395.

396.

397.

398.

399.

400.

401.

393. Your opponent attacks with a right kouchi-gari.

394–96. Slip your right leg free and throw him by twisting to your left.

397–401. Alternatively, twist and throw him to your right. You may also apply hiza-guruma.

Hane-goshi-gaeshi   Hip Spring Counter

402.

403.
408.

404.
409.

405.

402. Your opponent attacks with a right hane-goshi.

403–5. Hook your left leg around his lower left leg and reap it to your right.

406–9. Alternatively, lift him up and reap his legs to your left with your right leg.

Harai-goshi-gaeshi

410.   411.   412.   413.

Uchi-mata-gaeshi

416.   417.   418.   419.

Side Sacrifice Techniques

Kani-basami

422.   423.   424.   425.

Kawazu-gake

428.   429.   430.   431.

Hip Sweep Counter

410. Your opponent attacks with a right harai-goshi.

411–15. Hook your left leg around his lower left leg and reap it to your right.

414. 415.

Inner Thigh Reaping Throw Counter

416–21. When your opponent moves in for an uchi mata, hook your left leg around his left leg and reap it to your right.

420. 421.

Scissors Throw

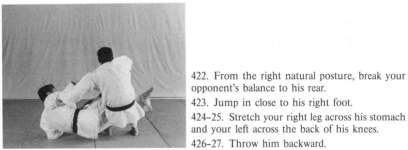

422. From the right natural posture, break your opponent's balance to his rear.

423. Jump in close to his right foot.

424–25. Stretch your right leg across his stomach and your left across the back of his knees.

426–27. Throw him backward.

426. 427.

One-Leg Entanglement

428. Step in on your opponent and slip your right arm around his neck.

429. Pivot and pull him tightly to you.

430. Wrap your right leg around the lower part of his left leg from the inside, pressing your instep against the back of his ankle.

431–33. Hook the leg up and throw yourself backward.

Note: This technique is not permitted in randori or tournaments.

432. 433.

Osoto-makikomi

434.   435.   436.   437.

434–36. From an osoto-gari or a similar technique, release your right grip and pivot to your left, bringing your right arm across your opponent's right arm so as to wrap his body around yours.

437–39. Continue turning and fall together.

Uchi-mata-makikomi

440.   441.   442.

440–45. From an uchi-mata, release your right grip and twist to your left, wrapping your opponent around you.

Harai-makikomi

446.   447.   448.

446–51. From harai-goshi, release your right grip and twist to your left, wrapping your opponent around you.

Large Outside Wraparound Throw

438.

439.

Inner Thigh Wraparound Throw

443.

444.

445.

Hip Sweep Wraparound Throw

449.

450.

451.

7. Katame-waza

The katame-waza introduced here are the ones most frequently used in randori and competition. In actual practice, a throw often precedes the grappling technique.

As noted in chapter 5, katame-waza consist of osae-komi-waza (hold-down techniques), shime-waza (strangling techniques) and kansetsu-waza (joint techniques).

Osae-komi-waza

In the descriptions that follow, techniques are executed with the opponent lying on his back on the mat. The right-handed forms are given here, but of course there are left-handed forms too.

In the hold-down techniques, the opponent is held in place from above. He is usually on his back and facing you. The objective is to get an unbroken hold, one that he cannot get out of within a fixed time limit.

The meaning of *unbroken* is that the opponent is unable to nullify the technique by gripping or seizing your trunk or legs with his legs.

Hon-kesa-gatame   Scarf Hold

Approaching your opponent from his right side and keeping your own body half turned to your left, you take his judogi at the right armpit in your left hand and put your right arm around his neck like a scarf, gripping his judogi at his left shoulder.

Be sure to keep your right hip and waist tight against your opponent's upper chest and armpit. Hold his right arm in your left armpit, close to your side.

1. Grab your opponent's upper right outer sleeve with your left hand and clamp his right arm in your left armpit. Put your right arm around his neck and place it either thumb up or palm down on the mat. Put your hip in his right armpit, bring your right thigh against the side of his body, and press the side of your body hard against his. Bend your left leg and stretch it out to your rear, then touch your head to the mat.

110

2. From your opponent's right side, trap his right arm in your left armpit and slip your right arm under his left armpit. Extend your right leg forward and your left leg backward. Use the right side of your body to apply pressure and hold him down.

3. With your left arm over your opponent's right shoulder and behind his neck, grip his left collar. Put your right thigh under the back of his head. Reach your right hand under his left armpit and grip the back of your right knee. Your left leg is stretched backward and you apply pressure mainly with the right side of your body on his right shoulder.

4. Hold your opponent's left arm with your left arm going over his left shoulder and under his left armpit. Take hold of the right side of his belt with your right hand. With your right leg extended forward and your left backward, press down on his left shoulder with the right side of your body.

Kuzure-kesa-gatame   Variation of Scarf Hold

These hold-down techniques are performed in ways that make them different from the basic hon-kesa-gatame, as shown in the illustrations.

Defense

The following techniques are effective against the different forms of *kesa-gatame.*

1. Grab your opponent's front belt with your right hand and his back belt with your left. Arch your body upwards and push him up. Twist your hips to your right, slide your right knee under his body, and hold him between your legs.
2. While twisting to your right and pushing with your left hand, pull your right arm free, then twist back to the left and roll on your side.
3. If your opponent reacts to the last technique by applying pressure to your left side, quickly twist to the left and roll him over to your left side.
4. Grab the back of your opponent's belt with your left hand, arch your back, and push him up over your head, then give an additional push and slip out from under him.

5.

5. Put your right arm around your opponent's neck, pull his right arm straight with your left hand, and press it against the right side of his neck.

6. Put your left arm around his shoulder and clasp your hands. Pull up with your arms and press down with your head and neck to lock his arm. Bring your right leg against the side of his body, keeping your knee and the ball of your foot on the mat. Put your left leg out to your left.

6.

Kata-gatame   Shoulder Hold

Approaching your opponent from his right side, your body half turned to your left, you put your right arm around both his neck and his right arm and clasp your hands together.

You may position your legs as in kesa-gatame. Instead of clasping your hands together, it is possible to hold your opponent's outer right middle sleeve with your left hand and your own left lapel with your right.

Defense

Most of the defenses against kesa-gatame will work with kata-gatame as well. Combine these with the following.

Grab the back of your opponent's belt with your free left hand. Twist your body to the left until you can clasp your hands together. Push your opponent so he rolls to his left. Turn onto your face and release your right arm from his hold. Turn over by pivoting on your head and shoulders and right yourself.

7.

8.

7–8. Kneel above your opponent's head. Reach under his arms and grab his belt on both sides with your hands, thumbs on the inside. Clamp his arms in the crooks of your arms while pressing the side of your head against his abdomen. Open your knees and bear down on him with your body.

9.

Kami-shiho-gatame   Top Four-corner Hold

While kneeling above your opponent's head, you grab his belt with both hands under his upper arms and press your body down on his.

Beginners should keep their insteps flat on the mat. (*Fig. 9*) Advanced students may kneel on the balls of their feet, which makes it easier to change positions if necessary. Be sure not to relax your grip on your opponent's belt. If he tries to raise a shoulder, shift your body and press down on it. Similarly control his other attempts to free himself with your arms and body pressure.

Defense

1. Make a space between your bodies by arching your back and pushing your opponent upward with both hands or by grabbing one of his legs with the opposite hand. Then either twist onto your stomach and slide yourself out from under him, or insert one or both knees into the gap and push him off you.

2. Grab one of his knees with either hand and rock him to the right and left until you can roll him off to the side opposite the leg you are holding.

3. Push your opponent's body up by straightening your arms, swing your legs up and clasp his body between them, then sit up.

10.   11.

12.

10–11. Kneel just behind your opponent's right shoulder. Slip your left arm underneath his left shoulder and grab his rear belt with your thumb on top. Put your right arm underneath his right armpit and grab the far corner of his rear belt. Spread your legs wide and slide back until your abdomen touches the mat. Draw your elbows to your sides to tighten your hold.

This technique is done slightly differently in the grappling kata. Put your right arm underneath your opponent's right armpit, take hold of his back collar with your right hand (thumb down) and hold his right arm tight against your body. Stay on your knees and bring them close to his shoulders, using your right knee to further control his right arm.

Kuzure-kami-shiho-gatame   Broken Top Four-corner Hold

This is a variation of kami-shiho-gatame. Your right hand should hold well past your left. (*Fig. 12*)

Defense

1. Arch your back and push your opponent upward with your hands to create an opening between your bodies. Push him away with your legs by either: bringing your feet up and placing them on his waist; putting your knee or toes under his shoulder; or twisting to the side, bending your body, and putting a leg under him. At the end of your counter move, you should be holding his body between your legs.

2. Pull with your left hand and push upward with your right, turn to your left, and try to roll your opponent over your body to your left.

In either case, if your opponent shifts his position from your right shoulder to your left, roll him over to your right.

Of greatest importance when attempting to escape from the kata form of kuzure-kami-shiho-gatame is freeing your right arm.

13.

14.

15.

13. Approach your opponent from his right side. With your right hand, reach around his left thigh and grab the back of his belt. Put your left arm around his neck and grab the top of his left lapel. Bring your right knee up against his hip. Your left leg can be straight back, ball of the foot on the mat, or you may bring your left knee up against his armpit. Press down strongly with your body, keeping your hips low, and hug him tightly.

14. Illustrated here is a variation of this technique called *kuzure-yoko-shiho-gatame* (broken side-locking four-corner hold). Reach over your opponent's left shoulder and grab the rear of his belt with your left hand.

15. Your right hand should hold his pants at the crotch so that you can pull and push with it in response to his movements.

Yoko-shiho-gatame   Side Locking Four-corner Hold

You hold your opponent down with your body at a right angle to his.

To prevent him from sliding his right leg between your bodies, place your right knee against his waist and press down on him with your body. If necessary, change the position of your hips and legs. It is also important that you control his upper body by squeezing with your left arm.

Defense

1. Grab the rear of your opponent's belt with your left hand and the front with your right, arch your back, and lift him up. At the same time, slip your right leg under his body and apply a scissors hold with your legs. If he resists your attempt to raise him, utilize his pushing force and roll him over to your left.

2. Apply an armlock to his left arm with your right.

3. Roll over onto your face before he can apply the hold.

16.

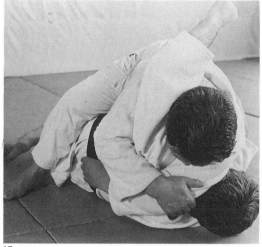

17.

16-17. Sit astride your opponent's chest, reach over his left shoulder with your left arm, and grab his rear belt. Pull his left arm straight with your right hand, then reach around the elbow and grab your left lapel, thereby trapping the arm between your right arm, shoulder and neck. (As an alternative, you may clasp your hands, trapping the arm between your left arm, shoulder and neck as in kata-gatame.)

18. Lean forward until your head is on the mat, and press down hard on your opponent with your chest. Put your feet as far under his hips or thighs as you can and squeeze his body with your knees.

18.

Tate-shiho-gatame   Straight Locking Four-corner Hold

Sitting astride your opponent's chest, you lay forward and press down on his upper body with your chest.

If possible, shift your body toward his left shoulder and press your left knee against his right ear. This is the most effective position. If he arches his back, quickly move your feet under his body and join them.

Defense

Using your right arm and legs, try to catch your opponent's left leg or both legs between your legs. As you arch your back, push up strongly, and roll him over to your left. Make a continuous effort to free your left arm.

19.

21.

20.

19. Sit astride your opponent's abdomen, your knees on the mat. Cross your arms and grip the tops of his lapels. Both hands should hold with the thumb inside.

20. While controlling his body with your legs, bend forward and pull with both hands, spreading your elbows.

Shime-waza

In strangulation techniques or choke locks, you use your hands, arms or legs on the opponent's collar or lapels to apply pressure to his neck or throat.

Nami-juji-jime   Normal Cross Lock

Crossing your arms, you grip your opponent's collar with both hands using the regular grip and put pressure on his neck as in the previous technique. (*Fig. 21*)

Be sure to control his body as you apply the technique. Practice so that you can grab the top of his lapels quickly and effectively.

This technique, too, can be applied while on your back, but only if you have your legs around your opponent so you can control him.

Defense

1. Twist to your right, get your left arm under your opponent's left arm, and place the palm of your left hand on the back of your neck.

2. Push his left elbow with your right hand or both elbows at the same time and roll him off to your left side.

22. With your arms crossed, grab high on your opponent's lapels with your thumbs on the outside. Twist your left wrist to the left and your right wrist to the right and pull with both arms so that the backs of your hands press against his carotid arteries.

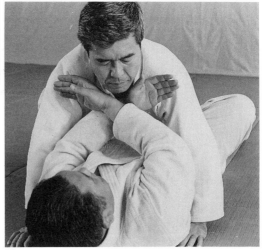

23.

Gyaku-juji-jime   **Reverse Cross Lock**

As in the previous technique, you hold your opponent's lapels or the back of his collar with your arms crossed and choke him by applying pressure with your hands.

Again, it is important that you control your opponent's body while you apply the technique. Either arm may be on top, but it is always the top arm that takes the normal grip. (*Fig. 23*)

This technique can be applied from above, from the sides, while on one's back, or while standing. Illustrated above is the supine version.

Defense

1. Push your opponent's elbows with your hands.
2. Push his right elbow with your left hand, twist your body to the left, insert your right hand underneath his right forearm, and place it behind your neck.

24.

25.

26.

24. Straddle your opponent's abdomen with your knees on the mat. Take the top of his left lapel in your left hand with your thumb outside. Grab his right lapel near his neck with your right hand, the fingers outside. Pull with your left hand and press with your right, letting your right elbow bend.

25. Preferably bend forward and press your right elbow against the mat. Put your strength into your arms and choke him as quickly as possible.

Kata-juji-jime   Half Cross Lock

While sitting atop your opponent, you take his left lapel in your left hand (thumb outside) and his right lapel in your right hand (fingers outside) and pull with your left hand and push with your right, as if wringing out a towel, to choke him. The grip with the thumb inside is the regular grip; with the fingers inside, it is the reverse grip. (*Fig. 26*)

To apply this technique, you must control your opponent with your knees and feet. Apply pressure to his neck with your left inner wrist and right outer wrist. The positions of your hands can be reversed, but in either case the hand on top must hold his lapel with the fingers outside.

Defense

Push your opponent's right elbow up with your left hand while pulling him with your right, and roll him off to your right side. You can roll him to your left, but in that case you must also stick your right hand under his right forearm and pry his hands loose, then place the palm of your hand behind his head. If your opponent is attacking you from the top or the side, break his grip with your left hand.

27. Kneel on the ball of your left foot behind your seated opponent. Your right knee should be just outside his right side. Put your right arm around his neck and bring the inside of your mid-forearm or the thumb side of your wrist up against it. Clasp your hands, left palm up, near his left shoulder. Put the right side of your head against the left side of his, and press his head toward your right arm. At the same time, pull him off balance to his back and pull hard against his windpipe with your right arm.

28. Illustrated here is a variation of hadaka-jime. Put your left arm around your opponent's throat and lay it in the crook of your right arm. Push his head forward with your right hand while pulling him back with your left arm.

Hadaka-jime   Naked Lock

This technique is applied from behind, and you do not hold your opponent's judogi. Kneeling on your left knee, you put your right inner arm against the front of his neck, clasp your hands above his left shoulder, and apply the pressure from the combined action of the arms to his throat.

Hadaka-jime can also be applied to an opponent who is standing or lying on the mat.

Defense

Grabbing the outside of your opponent's right sleeve at the shoulder with both hands, pull down hard, lean backward, and try to slip your head free.

29. While your opponent is lying on his back, slide underneath him and put your legs around him to control his movement. Put your right arm around his neck and grab his left lapel as high up as possible, with your fingers on the outside. Reach through his left armpit with your left hand and grab his right lapel, with your fingers on the outside. Arch backward, pulling back with your right hand and down with your left.

30. If your opponent is seated on the mat, place your forehead on the nape of his neck, break his balance to the rear, and apply the technique.

31. If he is lying on his stomach, reach in from the sides to grab his lapels, then bend forward over him as you apply pressure to his neck.

29.

30.

31.

Okuri-eri-jime   Sliding Collar Lock

You grip your opponent's upper left lapel from behind with your right hand and his right lapel with your left hand and choke him with both hands as if wringing his neck.

Instead of first reaching around his neck with your right arm, you can put your left arm through his left armpit, grab his left lapel, and pull it down, then grab it with your right. Your left hand then takes hold of his left lapel.

If your opponent resists by crossing his arms and holding his own lapels, put your right leg on his right shoulder and push his right hand off his lapel. Then trap his right arm by crossing your legs behind his back.

Defense

As in hadaka-jime, grab his right sleeve with both hands and pull down, then push it up to your left and slip your head free.

32.

33.

32. Your opponent is lying on the mat. Slide underneath him and control his body with your legs. Put your right arm around his neck and take hold of the top of his left lapel. Put your left hand through his left armpit and push his left arm up with your left forearm, then place your left hand, with the wrist and fingers straight, between his neck and your right arm. While pressing against his neck with your left hand, pull down hard on his left lapel with your right hand.

33. The use of your hands and arms is the same when you apply the technique to someone sitting or squatting. Your legs, however, should be positioned as in hadaka-jime. Be sure to break your opponent's balance to the rear.

Kata-ha-jime   Single-Wing Lock

From the rear, you put your right arm around your opponent's neck, grasping the top of his left lapel, then slip your left hand through his left armpit and up around the back of his neck—back of your left hand against the back of his neck. Choke him by pulling with your right hand and pushing with your left.

If you first pull his left lapel down with your left hand, you will find it easier to grab high with your right hand.

Defense

When your opponent is about to put his left hand behind your neck, pull it down with your right hand and bend your head backward.

34.

Katate-jime   One-Hand Choke

While holding the opponent down on his back, grasp his left collar from the side with your left hand, thumb inside. The technique is completed by applying pressure to his throat. (*Fig. 34*)

35.   36.

Ryote-jime   Two-Hand Choke

From the front, grip your opponent's right collar with your left hand, thumb inside, and his left collar with your right hand, thumb inside. Apply pressure to both sides of his neck with your fists. (*Figs. 35–36*)

37.

Sode-guruma-jime   Sleeve Wheel Choke

This technique is also applied from the front. Put your right forearm against your opponent's throat and your left forearm against the back of his neck. Grasp your right lower sleeve with your left hand and thrust your right hand into the right side of his neck. Apply pressure by making circular movements with both arms. (*Fig. 37*)

38.

39.

40.

Tsukkomi-jime   Thrust Choke

Grip your opponent's right collar (or both collars) from the front with your left hand. Thrust your right hand against the right side of his neck and apply pressure. (*Figs. 38–40*)

41.

Sankaku-jime   Triangular Choke

Apply pressure to your opponent's neck by wrapping your right leg over his left shoulder and your left leg under his right armpit. Catch your right foot under the back of his left knee in the diagonal *sankaku* position. Squeezing your legs will put pressure on the left side of his neck. (*Fig. 41*)

42.   43.

44.

42. As you approach your opponent from his right side, he raises his left hand and attempts to grab your lapel. Grab the inner side of his left wrist with your left hand, the back of your hand up, lean over him, and press his arm down outside his left shoulder. The elbow should be bent. Slip your right hand under his left upper arm and clasp your left wrist. While holding his wrist, apply pressure on his elbow by using your right forearm as a lever against the back of his left upper arm.

43. Lean over your opponent from his right side, take his left wrist in your right hand, and bend his arm until it forms a right angle. Reach under his upper arm with your left hand and grab your right wrist. While raising your shoulders, press his wrist down with your right hand and force his left elbow up with your left forearm.

44. The same lock can be applied while you are on your back.

Kansetsu-waza

Joint locks are directed against the opponent's joints, which are twisted, stretched or bent with the hands, arms or legs.

Ude-garami   Entangled Armlock

Taking your opponent's wrist in your left hand, you put your right forearm underneath his left upper arm and grab your own left wrist, then lock his elbow joint by pressing against his upper arm with your right forearm.

For the technique to be effective, you must control your opponent's left arm well and apply leverage efficiently.

Illustrated above are three ways of doing the technique.

Defense

1. To defend against the first form of the technique, grab your own left wrist with your right hand, turn your body to the left and stand up.

2. Against the second form, raise your upper body, grab your own belt or jacket with your left hand, and turn over to your left. If your opponent then tries to apply the technique from behind, stand before he can get his hands in place.

45.

46.

45. You are kneeling on your left knee to the right of your opponent. He reaches for your lapel with his right arm. Take it in your hands, placing both your palms on the inner side, your thumbs on the outside. Pull with both hands and place the front of your right shin up against his right side, then roll backward, dropping your hips as close to his shoulder as possible, and place your left leg over his throat and chest so that he cannot sit up. While holding the arm inner side up, lift your hips and pull down on the wrist with both hands.

46. The same technique can be applied while on one's back.

Ude-hishigi-juji-gatame   **Cross Armlock**

While holding your opponent's right wrist with both hands, you trap his right arm between your thighs and bend it back toward the elbow on the little-finger side.

This technique is generally applied on the mat, either when your opponent is still holding your left lapel or sleeve after you have thrown him, or when you approach him from his right side, kneeling on your left knee, and he grabs for your lapel with his right hand.

The same technique can be applied while on one's back.

Defense

1. With your left hand, grab your right wrist or lower right sleeve before your opponent can take hold of it, and twist and bend to your right.

2. If caught in this lock, turn and bend your right arm until your elbow points to the side, push your opponent's left leg away with your left hand, and roll your body to the left until it is parallel with your opponent's, then pull your arm free.

47. You are lying on your back. Your opponent reaches for you with his left arm. Quickly place the palm of your closed right hand or your forearm on or slightly above the back of his left elbow and press it down until his left wrist meets your right shoulder and his arm is straight.

48. Clasp your left hand over your right, and while controlling his body with your legs and twisting to your right, press down on his elbow with both hands.

49. You can also use this technique while standing, or on an opponent who is on his back. The time to apply it while standing is when your opponent rests his wrist on your upper arm.

47.

48.

49.

Ude-hishigi-ude-gatame   Arm Armlock

In this technique, also known as *ude-hishigi-zempaku-gatame*, you pull your opponent's left wrist against your right shoulder, place your hands or right forearm above the elbow of his outstretched arm, and press it down toward your body, bringing pressure to bear on his left elbow.

Defense

Instead of attempting to pull your arm free, push it past your opponent's shoulder and bend it.

50.

50. You are on your back. Your opponent reaches through your legs with his left hand. Quickly trap it in your right armpit and grab his right lapel with your left hand. Put your left foot against the upper part of his right thigh or groin and push, thereby breaking his balance forward.

51. Control him by bending your right leg and putting your foot a little above the left side of his belt. At the same time, twist your hips to your left, place the inner side of your right knee on the outside of his elbow, and press down hard.

51.

Ude-hishigi-hiza-gatame   Knee Armlock

You hold your opponent's right wrist in your left armpit and press down on his elbow from the outside with your left knee.

Coordinating three movements is of the utmost importance: push against the opponent's right side with your left foot, break his balance forward, and press his right elbow with your left knee.

Defense

1. Twist your right wrist clockwise and pull it out of your opponent's armpit.

2. Push your arm through his armpit to relieve the pressure on the elbow.

3. Roll forward over his body.

52.

Ude-hishigi-waki-gatame   **Armpit Armlock**

From the side, get a grip on one of your opponent's wrists with both hands and hold his arm in your armpit. Stretch his elbow and lock the straightened arm. (*Fig. 52*)

53.   54.

Ude-hishigi-hara-gatame   **Stomach Armlock**

Grip one of your opponent's wrists from the side, using either left or right hand. Then use your stomach or chest to apply pressure to his elbow. Lock the elbow by straightening, twisting or bending the arm. (*Figs. 53–54*)

55.

Ude-hishigi-ashi-gatame   **Leg Armlock**

With him face down and you to one side, catch your opponent's forearm with one leg. Straighten or bend the arm to lock the elbow. (*Fig. 55*)

Ude-hishigi-te-gatame Hand Armlock

From your opponent's right side, slip your left hand through his right armpit and grasp his left front collar. Take hold of his right wrist with your right hand, straighten his arm, and lock his elbow. (*Fig. 56*)

It is also possible to grasp his wrist with one or both hands and apply a lock to his elbow by twisting his arm behind his back. (*Fig. 57*)

58

Ude-hishigi-sankaku-gatame Triangular Armlock

Wrap one leg over your opponent's shoulder and the other under the opposite armpit to control his head in the diagonal sankaku-gatame. This can be done from the front, the side or the rear. Using one or both hands, either straighten or bend his trapped arm to get his elbow in a lock. (*Figs. 58–59*)

8. Continuous Attack

In randori and in tournament competition, continuous attacks occur frequently. Continuous attacks are of two kinds: combinations while on the offensive and counterattacks when the opponent's maneuver is unsuccessful.

It is not always possible to defeat an opponent with the application of a single technique. Sometimes you must use techniques in combination, for instance a throw followed by another throw. Or if you throw the opponent but fail to score a full point, you may want to move into a mat technique. This does not mean that once you have begun a technique you should not follow through. You should always make the utmost effort to be successful with every technique you apply, and toward that end you should study hard to master both tsukuri and kake. But in the event your technique fails, you must be ready to apply another without delay.

You must at all times be able to move smoothly into your own technique when attacked by your opponent. By counterattacking, you regain the initiative and prevent your opponent from continuing his attack.

As you advance in your study of judo, you will become aware of openings, the opportunities that occur naturally to apply combinations and counterattacks. That is an indication that you are beginning to grasp judo's underlying principle.

Below, under the two general categories of combinations and counterattacks, we have listed a few examples. An almost unlimited number of combinations is possible.

Combination Attacks
From throw to throw
In the same direction
Right *hiza-guruma* → right *hiza-guruma*
From right to left
Right *harai-tsurikomi-ashi* → left *harai-tsurikomi-ashi*
Right *hiza-guruma* → left *deashi-harai*

1–8. Right *hiza-guruma* to left *deashi-harai*.

1.   2.   3.   4.

   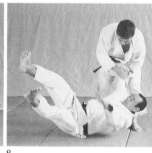

5.   6.   7.   8.

From front to back
Uchi-mata → *kouchi-gari*
Hane-goshi → *ouchi-gari*
From back to front
Ouchi-gari → *tai-otoshi*

9–16. *Ouchi-gari* to *kesa-gatame*.

9.   13.   10.   14.   11.   15.   12.   16.

Osoto-gari → *harai-goshi*

From throw to hold

Osoto-gari → *kesa-gatame*

17–24. *Osoto-gari* to *kesa-gatame*.

17.   18.   19.   20.

21.   22.   23.   24.

Tomoe-nage → *kuzure-kami-shiho-gatame*

From grappling technique to throw

Kata-juji-jime in standing position → *ouchi-gari*
Ude-hishigi-waki-gatame in standing position → *kouchi-gari*

From grappling technique to grappling technique

Kesa-gatame → *kata-gatame*
Okuri-eri-jime → *hadaka-jime*
Ude-hishigi-ude-gatame → *juji-gatame*
Kuzure-kami-shiho-gatame → *ude-hishigi-juji-gatame*
Yoko-shiho-gatame → *okuri-eri-jime*

25–32. *Yoko-shiho-gatame* to *okuri-eri-jime*.

25.   26.   27.   28.

29.　　　　30.　　　　　　31.　　　　　　32.

Kata-juji-jime → ude-hishigi-juji-gatame

Counterattacks

From throw to throw

Making use of your opponent's technique
Kouchi-gari → tomoe-nage
Kosoto-gari → uchi-mata

Taking advantage of his weakness when initiating a throw
Tomoe-nage → ouchi-gari
Hiza-guruma → ouchi-gari

Taking advantage of his weakness after he fails in his attack
Hane-goshi → hiza-guruma
Hane-goshi → hane-goshi

Controlling his technique
Hane-goshi → utsuri-goshi

33–40. *Hane-goshi* to *utsuri-goshi.*

33.　　　　34.　　　　　35.　　　　　　36.

37.　　　　38.　　　　　39.　　　　40.

134 CONTINUOUS ATTACK

Seoi-nage → *ura-nage*
Harai-goshi → *ushiro-goshi*

Avoiding then making use of his technique
Deashi-harai → *okuri-ashi-harai*
Uchi-mata → *tai-otoshi*

Attacking him as he attacks
Ouchi-gari → *okuri-ashi-harai*
Osoto-gari → *osoto-gari*

From throw to grappling technique

Tomoe-nage → *kesa-gatame*
Kata-guruma → *hadaka-jime* → *tate-shiho-gatame*
Uki-waza → *ude-hishigi-juji-gatame*
          → *ude-hishigi-hiza-gatame*
          → *tate-shiho-gatame*

From grappling technique to throw

Kata-juji-jime in standing position → *tomoe-nage*
Hadaka-jime in standing position → *seoi-nage*
Ude-hishigi-waki-gatame → *sukui-nage*

From grappling technique to grappling technique

All conceivable combinations of techniques are possible.

9. Atemi-waza

Respect for life is universally recognized, and if an individual's life is at stake, any means available to avert the danger is undeniably justified. Even when life is not threatened, the power to restrain others is a source of physical and psychological confidence.

In a society living under the rule of law and order, unwarranted and unreasonable attacks may come in the form of accidents, at the hands of criminals or from such unexpected quarters as a crazed dog on the loose. Each individual wants, therefore, to have the basic ability to defend himself, and it is the person who has as a matter of course trained himself in the techniques of attack and defense who can preserve his safety. The importance of atemi-waza in this respect is obvious.

While the throwing techniques of Kodokan judo are based on those of the Kito School, striking techniques are, like the grappling techniques, derived from those of the Tenshin Shin'yo School.

Atemi-waza are self-defense techniques in which attacks are made to the opponent's vital points to inflict pain, unconsciousness or death. They are employed only as a last resort when one is in danger of being killed, injured or captured. Striking between the eyes, or to the chest or solar plexus, and kicking to the groin are the most common techniques.

Unlike throwing and grappling techniques, striking techniques are never used in competition, due to the likelihood of injury. They are usually practiced in kata form.

The vast majority of atemi-waza are executed with parts of the arm or leg, although the head is sometimes used. They are classified as follows.

Atemi-waza

Leg		
Heel	Ball of Foot	Knee
Ushiro-geri Yoko-geri	Naname-geri Mae-geri Taka-geri	Mae-ate

Arm				
Elbow	Outside edge of Hand	Fist		Fingertip
Ushiro-ate	Kirioroshi Naname-uchi	Naname-ate Yoko-ate Kami-ate Tsukiage Shimo-tsuki Ushiro-tsuki	Ushiro-sumi-tsuki Tsukkake Yoko-uchi Ushiro-uchi Uchioroshi	Tsukidashi Ryogan-tsuki

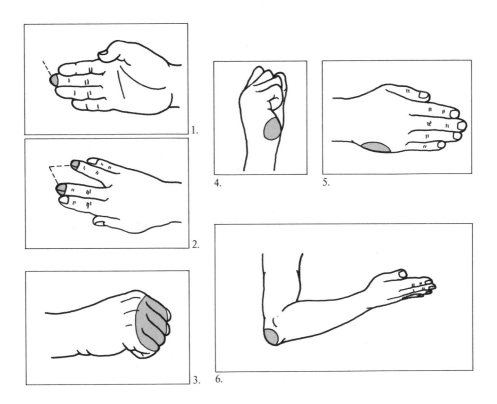

THE BODY'S WEAPONS

Although blows may be struck with various parts of the body, those shown in the table are the ones most commonly used. The following is a summary.

Fingertips

Strikes are made between the eyes with the middle finger (*tsukidashi*, *Fig. 1*) or to both eyes with the middle and ring fingers (*ryogan-tsuki, Fig. 2*).

Fist

The fist is formed with the thumb outside. Punches are delivered with the back of the fingers, keeping the wrist straight, or the knuckles, with the wrist bent. (*Fig. 3*) A downward blow is delivered with the padded area beneath the little finger, with the fist clenched and strength concentrated in the fourth and fifth fingers. (*Fig. 4*)

Knife Hand

The thumb and fingers are extended and held together. The blow is delivered with the padded area between the little finger and the wrist. (*Fig. 5*)

Elbow

The elbow is used to deliver a blow to the solar plexus of a person standing behind you. Before the strike, the hand is held palm up, thumb and fingers extended, and the forearm is kept horizontal to the ground. (*Fig. 6*)

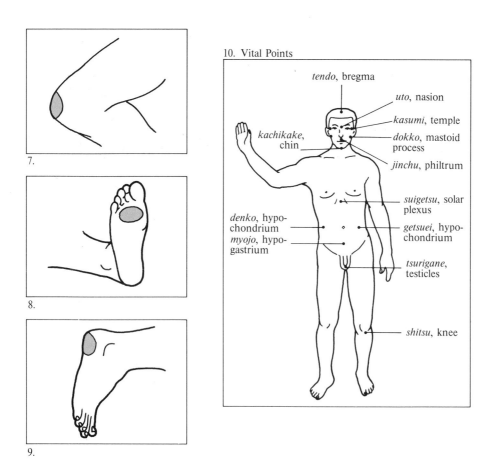

7.

8.

9.

10. Vital Points

tendo, bregma

uto, nasion

kasumi, temple

dokko, mastoid process

kachikake, chin

jinchu, philtrum

suigetsu, solar plexus

denko, hypo-chondrium

myojo, hypo-gastrium

getsuei, hypo-chondrium

tsurigane, testicles

shitsu, knee

Knee

Blows are struck directly to the front with the kneecap. (*Fig. 7*)

Ball of the Foot

Most kicks are made with the ball of the foot. The toes are raised and the movement comes from the hips. (*Fig. 8*)

Heel

Kicks are delivered with the bottom of the heel. (*Fig. 9*)

VITAL POINTS

The human body has numerous vital points: joints, points where bone and muscle connect or muscle meets muscle, soft areas unprotected by bone or muscle, and certain areas where vital organs are relatively close to the surface. In judo, like the striking techniques themselves, identification of the most vulnerable of these has been handed down from the Tenshin Shin'yo School. (*Fig. 10*)

III
FREE PRACTICE

10. Randori

1. *Randori* training in the Main Dojo of the Kodokan.

One reason judo has evolved into an international sport is that its two forms of practice, randori and kata, are ideal ways of training. This was not the case with jujutsu, which was learned almost exclusively through the practice of kata. In those schools that emphasized randori, such as the Kito and Tenshin Shin'yo schools, practice in randori came only after attaining proficiency in kata.

The origin of randori is in a type of training known as *nokori ai*, practiced shortly before the Meiji Restoration of 1868. A form of kata practice in which opponents executed a set series of techniques, the tori's throw had to be executed effectively or the uke would apply a counter throw. If the uke's counter throw was not effective, the tori might launch his own counterattack.

The ultimate goal of randori is to develop the ability to rapidly cope with changing circumstances, to build a strong and supple body, and to prepare mind and body for competition. To derive the maximum benefit from randori, it must be practiced in the way most likely to achieve results. Pay particular attention to the following three points:

1. The fundamental body position is, and must be, shizentai. This basic natural posture is not only the most adaptable to change but also the least tiring. Both partners take the same posture.

2. The emphasis is first on throwing techniques. Throwing practice is more valuable both as physical education and as spiritual training, since it requires perceiving and reacting to a greater range of situations. By moving on to grappling techniques only after extensive practice of throwing techniques, it is possible to become equally proficient at both. Those who specialize in judo over a number of years have ample opportunity to study in depth, but for anyone who might be tempted to learn one or the other, throwing techniques definitely take precedence. It is better to concentrate properly on one rather than treat inadequately with two. If groundwork is undertaken first, later chances to learn nage-waza may be few or non-existent. Especially if practice time is limited, concentration should be on learning throws.

3. Always keep in mind that randori is training in the art of attack and defense. In a martial art, it is essential to train the body to move freely and agilely to deal with punching and kicking attacks and to nurture the ability to react quickly and skillfully. The immediate goal is to win. Never admit defeat.

Unfortunately, in many dojo today randori is not practiced as it should be. One reason is the stress on training for competition. In tournament competition, participants tend to abandon the basic natural posture and assume stiff defensive postures. The resulting contest-style judo is far from ideal.

Practicing in the natural posture, points never to be neglected are: never use excess force, always put strength in shoulders, hips and limbs only as required, and always perform movements harmoniously in a controlled way, according to your own volition.

A second reason for current practices is that with the growth in the number of people practicing judo, there is a lack of qualified instructors worldwide and standards have been compromised. Reinstitution of Kodokan style randori is surely one of the most pressing tasks facing the judo world today.

IV
FORMS

11. Kata

The following are seven types of kata (prearranged forms) taught today at the Kodokan.

Randori no Kata (Free Exercise Forms), consisting of:
Nage no Kata (Throwing Forms)
Katame no Kata (Grappling Forms)
Kime no Kata (Forms of Decision)
Kodokan Goshin Jutsu (Kodokan Self-defense Forms)
Ju no Kata (Forms of Gentleness)
Itsutsu no Kata (The Five Forms)
Koshiki no Kata (Ancient Forms)
Seiryoku Zen'yo Kokumin Taiiku no Kata (Maximum-Efficiency National Physical Education Kata)

In this chapter we will briefly outline all but the last one. Each kata is in essence a selection of model techniques. Practice of techniques as they occur in the kata will help in understanding the theoretical basis of judo.

Nage no Kata

The Nage no Kata consists of fifteen representative techniques, three from each of the five categories of throwing techniques.

TABLE I

Te-waza	Koshi-waza	Ashi-waza
Uki-otoshi	Uki-goshi	Okuri-ashi-harai
Seoi-nage	Harai-goshi	Sasae-tsurikomi-ashi
Kata-guruma	Tsurikomi-goshi	Uchi-mata

Ma-sutemi-waza		Yoko-sutemi-waza
Tomoe-nage		Yoko-gake
Ura-nage		Yoko-guruma
Sumi-gaeshi		Uki-waza

Katame no Kata

There are fifteen techniques in Katame no Kata, five from each of the three categories.

TABLE II

Osae-komi-waza	Shime-waza	Kansetsu-waza
Kesa-gatame	Kata-juji-jime	Ude-garami
Kata-gatame	Hadaka-jime	Ude-hishigi-juji-gatame
Kami-shiho-gatame	Okuri-eri-jime	Ude-hishigi-ude-gatame
Yoko-shiho-gatame	Kata-ha-jime	Ude-hishigi-hiza-gatame
Kuzure-kami-shiho-gatame	Gyaku-juji-jime	Ashi-garami

Kime no Kata

Kime no Kata is also known as *Shinken Shobu no Kata* (Combat Forms) and is designed to teach the fundamentals of attack and defense in an actual combat situation, as both names imply. Its twenty techniques, which include strikes at vital spots, are all applicable in real-life situations, but are banned in randori. They are divided into two groups, *idori*, where the basic position is kneeling, and *tachiai*, where techniques are executed in a standing position.

TABLE III

Idori	Tachiai	
Ryote-dori	Ryote-dori	Tsukkomi
Tsukkake	Sode-tori	Kirikomi
Suri-age	Tsukkake	Nuki-kake
Yoko-uchi	Tsukiage	Kirioroshi
Ushiro-dori	Suri-age	
Tsukkomi	Yoko-uchi	
Kirikomi	Keage	
Yoko-tsuki	Ushiro-dori	

Kodokan Goshin Jutsu

Kodokan Goshin Jutsu, formally established in 1958, is a set of twenty-one self-defense techniques, twelve for use against an unarmed assailant, nine against an armed assailant.

TABLE IV

Against Unarmed Attack	
When held	At a distance
Ryote-dori	Naname-uchi
Hidari-eri-dori	Ago-tsuki
Migi-eri-dori	Gammen-tsuki
Kataude-dori	Mae-geri
Ushiro-eri-dori	Yoko-geri
Ushiro-jime	
Kakae-dori	

Against Armed Attack		
Knife	Stick	Pistol
Tsukkake	Furiage	Shomen-zuke
Choku-zuki	Furioroshi	Koshi-gamae
Naname-zuki	Morote-zuki	Haimen-zuke

Ju no Kata

The movements in these forms are, as the name suggests, gentle. The exercises are designed to train one how to manage the body in an emergency and how to employ one's strength most effectively. Because their practice serves to condition the body and teach the concept of ju they are recommended to beginners. There are three sets, each of five techniques.

TABLE V

Set 1	Set 2	Set 3
Tsukidashi	Kirioroshi	Obi-tori
Kata-oshi	Ryokata-oshi	Mune-oshi
Ryote-dori	Naname-uchi	Tsukiage
Kata-mawashi	Katate-dori	Uchioroshi
Age-oshi	Katate-age	Ryogan-tsuki

Itsutsu no Kata

The five techniques in this kata are known only by number. The first two resemble jujutsu techniques, but the appearance of the other three, while intriguing, is unlike anything seen in jujutsu. The graceful movements are evocative of the motion of water, the heavenly bodies and other natural forces. The kata is considered unfinished.

Koshiki no Kata

Also known as the *Kito-ryu no Kata*, the twenty-one techniques in this kata were originally the Kito School's forms of throwing. I revised and incorporated them into Kodokan Judo. The techniques are of a high order and highly refined, and their practice brings insight into judo theory. The kata has two parts.

TABLE VI

Omote		Ura
Tai	Uchikudaki	Mi-kudaki
Yume-no-uchi	Tani-otoshi	Kuruma-gaeshi
Ryokuhi	Kuruma-daore	Mizu-iri
Mizu-guruma	Shikoro-dori	Ryusetsu
Mizu-nagare	Shikoro-gaeshi	Sakaotoshi
Hikiotoshi	Yudachi	Yukiore
Ko-daore	Taki-otoshi	Iwa-nami

12. Nage no Kata

Nage no Kata is the first of the two Randori no Kata. Its fifteen techniques are given in Table I on page 145.

To begin the kata, you (tori) and your partner (uke) stand facing each other at a distance of about 5.5 meters. (*Fig. 1*) You should be on the right as seen from the *joseki*. Both turn toward the *joseki* and perform a standing bow, then turn and face each other and do a kneeling bow. (*Figs. 2–3*) (The meaning of *joseki* is "seat of honor." This side of the dojo is also designated as *shomen*, "front.")

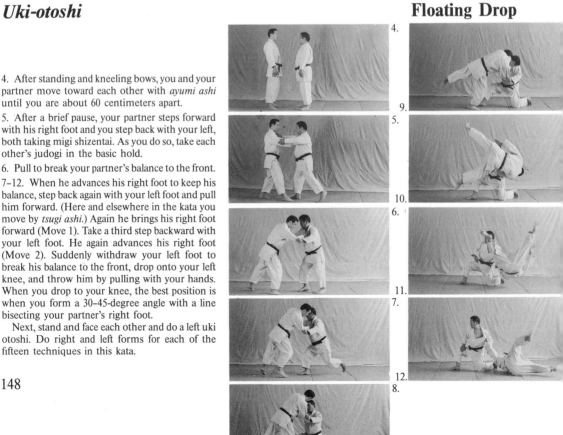

1. 2. 3.

HAND TECHNIQUES

Uki-otoshi

Floating Drop

4. After standing and kneeling bows, you and your partner move toward each other with *ayumi ashi* until you are about 60 centimeters apart.

5. After a brief pause, your partner steps forward with his right foot and you step back with your left, both taking migi shizentai. As you do so, take each other's judogi in the basic hold.

6. Pull to break your partner's balance to the front.

7-12. When he advances his right foot to keep his balance, step back again with your left foot and pull him forward. (Here and elsewhere in the kata you move by *tsugi ashi*.) Again he brings his right foot forward (Move 1). Take a third step backward with your left foot. He again advances his right foot (Move 2). Suddenly withdraw your left foot to break his balance to the front, drop onto your left knee, and throw him by pulling with your hands. When you drop to your knee, the best position is when you form a 30–45-degree angle with a line bisecting your partner's right foot.

Next, stand and face each other and do a left uki otoshi. Do right and left forms for each of the fifteen techniques in this kata.

4.

9.

5.

10.

6.

11.

7.

12.

8.

Seoi-nage

13.

14.

15.

16.

17.

18.

19.

20.

21.

13. After returning to your original position, approach each other until you are about 1.8 meters apart.

14. Your partner steps forward with his left foot and raises his right fist.

15. He comes forward with his right foot and aims a downward blow at the top of your head with the base of his right fist. Step forward to put your right foot inside his right foot. Utilizing his movement, block the blow—your left inner forearm against his forearm.

16. Take hold of his right middle inner sleeve with your left hand to break his balance forward. Pivot to your left on your right toes and slip your right arm through his right armpit.

17. Grab his upper arm below the right shoulder. Continue turning to your left, bringing your left foot inside his left foot, and pull him tight against your back.

18-21. To throw, lift him, straighten your legs, and bend forward, bringing your hands down in front of you.

Kata-guruma　　　　　　　　　　　　　　　　**Shoulder Wheel**

22.　　　　　　23.　　　　　　　　24.　　　　　　25.

26.　　27.　　　　　　　28.　　　　　　29.

22. Approach to face each other at a distance of about 60 centimeters.

23. While taking each other in the basic hold, you step back into the right natural posture to break your partner's balance to the front. He comes forward with his right foot (Move 1).

24. Step back again with your left foot (tsugi-ashi), and switch your left grip from the elbow to the right middle inner sleeve, your arm under his. Pull to break his balance forward. He advances his right foot again (Move 2). Take one more big step back with your left foot while pulling with your left hand. As your partner comes forward again with his right foot, lower your hips until you are in jigotai.

25. As his balance breaks, bend forward, pressing your neck and right shoulder against his right hip, and circle his right thigh with your right arm from the inside.

26–27. While pulling him forward with your left hand, bring your left foot toward your right and, in a single integrated movement, stand, lifting him on your shoulders.

28–30. Throw him to your left front corner.

30.

Harai-goshi

41.　　　　　　42.　　　　　　　43.

40.

40–41. When you and your partner are about 60 centimeters apart, he moves his right foot forward and you step back with your left and take the basic hold.

42. Step back with your left foot and pull him

slightly forward. He reacts by stepping forward with his right foot (Move 1), and you step back again with your left foot.

43. Slip your right hand through his left armpit, and place it against his left shoulder blade. Pull and

Uki-goshi   ## Floating Hip Throw

31.

32.

33.

34.

35.

36.

37.   38.

39.

31. You and your partner advance to within 1.8 meters of each other.

32-34. He steps forward with his left foot and raises his right fist, advances on his right foot and attempts to strike the top of your head with the base of his fist. Before the blow connects, step to your right front corner with your left foot.

35. Lower your left shoulder slightly and bend to put your left arm under your partner's right and around his waist.

36. Pull him tight against you, breaking his balance to the front.

37-39. With your right hand, grip his left middle outer sleeve and twist to your right to throw.

Hip Sweep

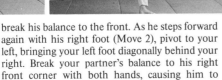
44.   45.   46.

break his balance to the front. As he steps forward again with his right foot (Move 2), pivot to your left, bringing your left foot diagonally behind your right. Break your partner's balance to his right front corner with both hands, causing him to

advance a small step with his right foot. Press your right hip firmly against his lower abdomen.

44-46. Throw him by sweeping upward against his right leg with your right leg.

Tsurikomi-goshi   **Lift-Pull Hip Throw**

47.   48.   49.   50.

51.   52.   53.   54.

55.

47. Approach to within 60 centimeters of each other.

48. When he moves his right foot forward and takes the basic hold, you move your left foot back and your right hand grips the back of his collar.

49. Pull to break his balance to the front, causing him to come forward with his right foot. Step back again with your left foot and pull him off balance. When he again comes forward with his right foot, take a small step back with your left foot and pull him forward.

50. As he advances his right foot, slide your right foot in front of his and pull him upward with your right hand. He brings his left foot forward and assumes a natural stance, straightening up to keep his balance. Pull him forward with your hands and pivot to your left, bringing your left foot inside his left foot. Lower your hips and press them against his thighs.

51–55. To throw, straighten your legs to raise your hips and pull down with your hands.

FOOT AND LEG TECHNIQUES

Okuri-ashi-harai

56.   57.   58.   59.

56–57. From a distance of 30 centimeters, you and your partner take the basic hold.

58. Take the initiative and move your right foot one step to the right and your left foot along with it,

forcing him to move with you to his left.

59. Repeat the move, lifting up with your hands as you do so.

60. As you take a third, big step to the right, lift up

Sasae-tsurikomi-ashi Supporting Foot Lift-Pull Throw

64.

65.

66.

67.

68.

69.

70.

64–65. At a distance of 60 centimeters, you take hold of each other's judogi in the basic hold. Your partner comes forward with his right foot and you move back on your left.

66. Try to break his balance forward.

67. When he reacts by stepping forward with his right foot, take another step back. He advances again.

68. Step back with your left foot and immediately move your foot to your right back corner. Turn your body to the left, right toes inward. When your partner tries to balance by coming forward with his right foot, apply the sole of your left foot to his right ankle and pull him upward.

69–72. Throw him forward by pulling strongly with your left hand and pushing with your right.

71.

72.

Foot Sweep

60.

61.

62.

63.

toward the right in a curving, diagonal movement. At the same time concentrate strength in the outer edge of your left foot and sweep your partner's trailing right outer ankle with your left sole.

61–63. Throw him in the direction he is moving.

Uchi-mata

73.　74.　　　　　75.　　　　　76.　　　　　77.　　　　　78.

73-74. Approach to about 60 centimeters and take the right natural posture and the basic hold.

75. While pulling with your right hand, step to your left front corner with your left foot and bring your right foot back to your left back corner.

76. Your partner comes forward in an arc, left foot first, then right.

77. Move in the same way to your left once more, leading your part-

SUPINE SACRIFICE TECHNIQUES

Tomoe-nage
Circular Throw

84.　85.　　　　　86.　　　　　87.　　　　　88.　　　　　89.

90.　　　　　91.　　　　　92.

84-85. Facing each other at 60 centimeters, both take the right natural posture and the basic hold.

86. Take three steps forward, beginning with your right foot, and try to break your partner's balance to the rear.

87. After retreating three steps, he resists by pushing back. At that moment, place your left foot inside his right foot, switch your left grip under his armpit to his right lapel, and break his balance to the front.

88. As he brings his left foot forward and his feet become parallel, bend your right leg, and lightly place your right foot (toes up) on his lower abdomen.

89-93. Sit down as close to your left heel as possible, and throw him up over your head by straightening your right leg and pulling in a downward arc with both hands.

93.

Inner Thigh Reaping Throw

79.   80.   81.   82.   83.

ner in a wide circular movement to his own right back corner.

78. As he is about to shift his weight to his left foot, break his balance to the front with both hands.

79. Lower your body, stick your right leg in between his legs, and twist to your left.

80–83. Lift, and throw him by reaping with your right leg up against the inside of his left thigh.

Ura-nage   Back Throw

94.   95.   96.   97.   98.

  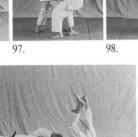

99.   100.   101.   102.

94–95. When you and your partner are about 1.8 meters apart, he aims a blow at your head with the base of his right fist.

96. Avoid the blow by extending your left foot well behind him.

97. Lower your hips and put your left arm around his waist.

98. Simultaneously bring your right foot up between his feet and place the palm of your right hand (fingers up) on his lower abdomen.

99–103. Keeping a tight grip on him, fall backward and throw him up over your left shoulder with the action of your hips and arms.

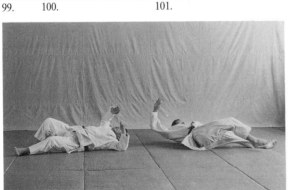

103.

104.   105.   106.

107.   108.   109.   110.

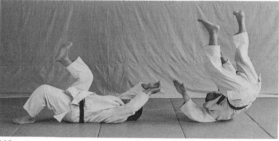

111.   112.

113.

114.

104. You and your partner advance to within 90 centimeters of each other.

105. Step forward with your right feet and engage in the right defensive posture, slipping your right hands through each other's armpits and placing the palms on each other's backs. Your left hands grasp the right outer elbows.

106. While pulling strongly upward with your right hand, take a big step back with your right foot, causing your partner to come forward with his left foot. As he tries to straighten up, lift upward with both hands. To keep his balance, he brings his right foot diagonally forward.

107–8. When his feet are parallel with each other, slide your left foot close to your right, and break his balance forward.

109–114. Throw yourself backward. As you fall, apply your right instep behind your partner's left knee and throw him up over your head with the combined action of your right leg and your arms.

SIDE SACRIFICE TECHNIQUES

Yoko-gake   **Side Body Drop**

115.

116.

117.

118.

119.

120.

121.

122.

115. Face your partner at a distance of about 60 centimeters.

116. He steps forward with his right foot and you take each other's judogi in the basic hold.

117. Step back with your left foot and attempt to break his balance to the front, causing him to bring his right foot forward. Take another step back with your left foot and make him advance his left foot, forcefully breaking his balance to his right front corner and tilting his body to the right.

118. Your partner advances his right foot again. Take a small step back with your right foot, and as he starts to come forward again with his right foot, bring your right foot up next to your left and again strongly break his balance to his right front corner with both hands.

119–22. At the same time, put your left sole against his right ankle and fall to your left, sweeping the ankle as you fall. Your left arm pulls and your right arm pushes in an arc.

Yoko-guruma

123.   124.   125.

130.   131.   132.

Uki-waza   **Floating Throw**

139.

134.   135.   136.   137.   138.
                140.   141.

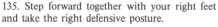

134. You and your partner approach and face each other at a distance of 90 centimeters.

135. Step forward together with your right feet and take the right defensive posture.

136. Lift your partner upward with your right hand and take a big step back with your right foot, causing him to step forward with his left foot.

137. Lift him with both hands. To keep his bal-ance, he steps to his right front corner with his right foot.

138. As he does so, straighten and slide your left leg in an arc toward his right back corner so as to block the foot, and fall onto your left side, pulling with your left hand and pushing with your right.

139–41. Your partner is thrown over his own right shoulder.

126.   127.   128.   129.

133.

123–25. From a position about 1.8 meters apart, your partner comes three steps toward you—left foot first—and aims the base of his right fist at the top of your head.

126. You attempt to throw him with ura-nage.

127. He counters by bending over.

128. Take advantage of his posture by breaking his balance to the front with your left hand and thrusting your right leg deep between his legs.

129–33. At the same time, throw yourself onto your right side, pulling with your left hand and pushing with your right, and throw your partner over your left shoulder.

142.   143.

144.   145.

After completing the series with a left uki-waza, you and your partner return to your starting positions. (*Fig. 142*) Facing each other, take the basic natural posture. In unison, move one step backward, right feet first. (*Fig. 143*) Once again at a distance of 5.5 meters, perform kneeling bows. (*Fig. 144*) Simultaneously stand, turn to face the joseki, and do standing bows. (*Fig. 145*)

13. Katame no Kata

Katame no Kata, the second of the Randori no Kata, is made up of three sets of techniques: osae-komi-waza, shime-waza and kansetsu-waza. The five representative techniques in each set are given in Table II on p. 145.

To begin the kata, you, the tori, and your partner, the nage, stand facing each other at a distance of about 5.5 meters. (*Fig. 1*) You should be on the right as seen from the joseki. Turn together toward the joseki and do a standing bow, then face each other and perform a sitting bow. (*Figs. 2–4*)

Stand and step forward with your left foot into shizentai. (*Fig. 5*) Withdraw your left foot and kneel on your left knee, instep off the mat. Angle your right knee toward the right front corner, and place your right hand on it. Your left hand should hang naturally. This is called *kyoshi*, the high kneeling posture. (*Fig. 6*)

Your partner shifts his right foot inward, then advances his right foot and brings his left knee up behind him. He moves his right knee outward again to resume the high kneeling posture. (*Fig. 7*) This method of moving on one knee is called *shikko*.

1.
2.
3.
4.
5.
6.
7.

160

8. 9.   10.

Osae-komi-waza

Each of the three sections of the kata begins with your partner assuming a prone position, as follows.

He places his right hand on the mat in front of his left knee with the fingers turned inward and to the left. (*Fig. 8*) Supporting his body on his right hand and left foot, he raises his left knee, turns to his left, and extends his right leg straight through the arch formed by his body. He rests his hips on the mat near his left heel with his left knee raised, lays back, and puts his hands on his body near his belt. (*Figs. 9–10*)

Each technique ends with your partner signalling defeat by patting you or the mat twice or, when neither hand is free, by hitting the mat twice with either foot.

Kesa-gatame   **Scarf Hold**

11.   12.   16.   13.   17.   14.

15.

11. Pull your right foot in and stand, then approach your partner with ayumi ashi until you are about 1.2 meters apart. Assume the high kneeling posture. This place is known as the "far position."

12. Continue your approach by *shikko* and stop when you are about 30 centimeters apart. This is the "near position."

13. Move slightly forward, take your partner's right hand in your hands and lift it. Next, take his right upper sleeve in your left hand and trap his arm under your arm.

14–15. While turning your body to the left, put your right knee into his right armpit and pass your right hand under his left armpit, placing it on his right shoulder. Lower yourself onto your right hip and press the right side of your chest down on his right chest. At the same time, extend your left leg behind you, bending it at the knee, and grip the mat with your toes. Extend your right leg forward with the knee bent.

16. Apply the hold by pulling strongly with your left hand.

17. Your partner goes through the motions of attempting to escape by various means, such as putting his arms around your waist and trying to roll you backward, inserting his right knee between your bodies, or bridging and throwing you forward. After a few seconds he stops moving and signals defeat. Release him and return to the near position, then the far position.

18.

19.

20.

21.

22.

23.

24.

18. Advance to the near position and from there move forward a bit more and lift your partner's right arm with both hands.

19. Push the arm toward his right ear with your right hand on the elbow and your left hand on the shoulder.

20. Move your right knee forward and press it against his right side. The instep of your right foot should be off the mat.

21. With your right hand, reach over his left shoulder and around under his neck to his right shoulder. Press his right arm against his right temple by

putting your right temple against his right arm, and clasp your hands together, palm against palm. Then straighten your left leg, gripping the mat with your toes. Tighten your grip to apply the hold.

22-24. Your partner attempts to escape, for example, by joining his hands together and pushing with his elbows to loosen your hold, by twisting to the right and slipping his right knee under your hip, or by rolling backward over his left shoulder. After a few seconds he signals defeat. Release your hold, return to the near position, then to the far position.

25.

26.

27.

28.

29.

30.

25. Move to the far position above your partner's head, then move to the near position.

26. ·Move closer, lower your right knee, and slide your hands under his shoulders.

27. Take his belt at both sides and trap his arms in your elbows, then press your chest down on his, causing his head to turn to one side. Apply the hold by lowering your hips.

28–30. Your partner attempts to escape by, for example, clasping his hands together, pushing your head to one side, and turning on his side; inserting his arms between your bodies and twisting to the side; or pushing you up and slipping his knees or feet between your bodies. Unable to escape, he signals defeat, whereupon you return to the near position, then the far position above his head.

Yoko-shiho-gatame

31. 32. 33.

Kuzure-kami-shiho-gatame ## Broken Top Four-corner Hol

37. 38. 39.

40. 41.
42. 43. 44.

37. Move to the far position above your partner's head, then move to the near position. Advance a little more, until your right foot is near his right shoulder.

38. Take his right arm from the inside with your right hand and lift it, then change hands, holding it with your left.

39. Bring you right knee up, slide your right hand under his back from his right armpit, and grasp the back of his collar. Hold his right arm tight against your thigh.

40. Slip your left hand under his left shoulder and grab his belt at the left side. Apply the hold by lowering your hips and pressing your chest against his right chest.

41–44. Your partner attempts to escape by, for example, pushing the side of your head with his left hand, turning to the right and pulling his right arm free; drawing up his left knee and inserting it between your bodies; or taking your belt at the rear and rolling you forward. Unable to escape, he signals defeat. Release your hold and return to the near position, then the far position. Meanwhile, your partner sits up, placing his right hand on the mat behind his right hip. Supporting himself on his left foot and right hand, he lifts his hips, turns to the right, and draws his right leg back so that he ends up in the high kneeling posture facing you.

34.   35.   36.

31. Move to the far position on your partner's right, then move to the near position. Move forward a bit more, pick up your partner's right hand in both hands and lay it down to your left. Move closer still and put your left knee into his right armpit. The instep of your left foot should remain off the mat.

32. With your left hand take your partner's right side belt and lower your right knee. Pass your right hand through his legs and grab his left side belt.

33. Put your left hand under his neck and grip his left collar. Press your left knee into his right armpit and your right knee against his right hip, and turn your head to the left to apply the hold.

34–36. Your partner tries to escape by, for instance, pushing your head back with his left hand and hooking your head with his left leg, twisting to his right and slipping his right knee under you, or grabbing the back of your belt with his left hand and rolling you forward. Unsuccessful, he signals defeat and you release your hold, move back to the near position, then to the far position.

Shime-waza

Kata-juji-jime

Half-cross Lock

45.   46.   47.

48.   49.

45. Move to the far position at the right of your partner, then advance to the near position.

46. Approach your partner, take his right arm in your hands, and lay it to your left. Move closer and take the top of his left lapel with your left hand, thumb outside.

47. Push his left arm away with your right hand and straddle him, squeezing and controlling his body with your legs.

48. Take the top of his right lapel with your right hand, thumb inside. Both your wrists should now be against your partner's throat.

49. Apply the choke by leaning forward and pulling with your left hand and pushing with your right.

Your partner tries to escape by pushing against your arms, then signals defeat. Return to the near position, then to the far position.

Hadaka-jime

50.

51.

Okuri-eri-jime

54.

56.

Sliding Collar Lock

55.

57.

54. Move up close to your partner.

55. Reach under his left armpit with your left hand and pull his left lapel down.

56. Reach around his neck with your right hand and grab high up on his left lapel. Take his right lapel with your left hand, put your right cheek against his left cheek, and press against the back of his neck with your right front shoulder.

57. Lower your body by drawing your left leg back, and break his balance to the rear. Apply the choke by putting pressure on his neck with your right hand while pulling down with your left and twisting to your right.

Your partner attempts to escape by pushing up on your right arm with his hands, then signals defeat. Release your hold and return to the near position behind him.

Naked Lock

52.

50. Your partner sits up and bends his left leg half-way. His right leg is slightly bent. Move to the far position behind him.

51. Proceed to the near position.

52. Move forward until you are directly behind him. Put your right arm around his neck and clasp your hands over his left shoulder, pressing the thumb side of your right wrist against his throat. Put your right cheek against his left cheek.

53. Lower your body by drawing your left leg back, and break his balance to the rear. Increase the pressure against his neck.

Your partner tries to escape by pushing your right arm up with both hands. then gives the signal of defeat. Release him and return to the near position at his rear.

53.

Kata-ha-jime   Single-Wing Lock

58.

59.

60.

61.

62.

58. Move up close to your partner.

59. Reach under his left armpit and pull down on his left lapel. Reach around his neck with your right hand and grab high up on his left lapel.

60. While breaking his balance to the rear, bring your left arm up, pushing his left arm up with it.

61. Lay the palm of your left hand, fingers straight, on the nape of his neck.

62. Shift your right foot and body slightly to the right. Pull with your right hand to apply the choke.

Your partner tries to escape by taking hold of his left wrist with his right hand and lifting his left arm, then signals defeat. Release your hold and return to the near position, then the far position.

63.   64.   65.

66.   67.

68.   69.

63. While your partner lies down again, you move to the far position at his right, then advance to the near position.

64. Move close to your partner, pick his right arm up with both hands, and place it on the mat to your left.

65. Move closer and grab high on his left lapel with your left hand, thumb outside.

66. Push his left arm away from you with your right hand and straddle him, controlling his movement with your legs. Take the top of his right lapel with your right hand, thumb outside.

67. Pull with both hands and lean forward to apply the choke.

68. Your partner tries to break the hold by pushing your left elbow from above with his right hand and your right elbow from underneath with his left hand. Roll onto your left side and cross your legs at the ankles, holding his body tightly between your legs. Continue to apply the technique. Unable to break the hold, your partner signals defeat.

69. Release your hold, return to the near position, then move back to the far position. Your partner sits up and assumes the high kneeling posture facing you.

Kansetsu Waza

Ude-garami   Entangled Armlock

70.

71.

72.

73.

74.

70. Move to the near position.

71. Move closer to your partner and with both hands pick up his right arm and place it to your left, then come closer still.

72. He tries to grab your right lapel with his left hand. Take his left wrist with your left hand, thumb down.

73. Lower your right knee to the mat, then bend his left arm at a right angle and press it to the mat near his left shoulder.

74. Use your right hand to reach under his left upper arm and grab your left wrist from the top. Put pressure on the elbow by drawing his wrist toward you and at the same time pressing your chest down on his.

Unable to escape, your partner gives the signal of defeat. Release his arm and return to the near position at his right.

Ude-hishigi-juji-gatame   Cross Armlock

75.

76.

77.

78.

79.

75. Move forward to attack your partner.

76. He tries to grab your left lapel with his right hand.

77. Take his right wrist in both hands, your right hand above your left, pull up, and move your right foot into his right armpit.

78. Bend forward and swing your left foot over his head in an arc, placing the sole of your left foot on the mat above his left shoulder. Trap his right upper arm between your thighs.

79. Sit down near your right heel and lie back. While controlling your partner's head with your left leg, bring your knees together and raise your hips to put pressure against his right elbow.

Unable to escape, he signals defeat. Release his arm and return to the near position.

Ude-hishigi-ude-gatame

80.

81.

82.

Ude-hishigi-hiza-gatame   **Knee Armlock**

86.

87.

88.

89.

90.

91.

92.

93.

94.

86. You and your partner advance to the near position.

87. You both continue forward and engage in the right basic hold.

88–89. Let go of your partner's right sleeve with your left hand. Slip the hand under his right arm then back over it, and place the palm of your left hand on the outside of the arm, slightly above the elbow. Trap his right wrist in your left armpit.

90. Break his balance to the front with both hands.

91. Put the toes of your right foot on his left hip at the joint and fall backward.

92. As you fall, put your left foot on the rear of his right hip.

93. Press the inside of your left knee against your left hand and twist your hips to the right to apply the lock.

Your partner tries to pull his left arm free, but unable to escape, he gives up.

94. Release his arm and return to the near position. Your partner sits up and faces you in the high kneeling posture.

Arm Armlock

83.

84.

85.

80. Move forward, pick up your partner's right arm with both hands and lay it on the mat to your right. Continue moving forward as if to attack him.

81. He reaches across with his left arm and tries to grab your right lapel. Lower your body and trap his left wrist between your neck and right shoulder.

82. Put the palm of your right hand on his left elbow and lay your left hand over your right. Press your right shin against his lower ribs while controlling the arm.

83. Twist to your left and put pressure against the elbow.

Your partner tries to escape by pulling his left arm free. Unable to escape, he signals defeat.

84. Release his arm and return to the near position, then to the far position.

85. From there move to the far position above your partner's head. At the same time, your partner sits up, turns, and faces you in the high kneeling posture.

Ashi-garami   ## Entangled Leglock

95.

96.

97.

98.

100.

99.

95. You and your partner stand, approach each other, and engage in the basic hold.

96. Break your partner's balance to the front with both hands, put your left foot in between his legs, fall backward, and place the sole of your right foot on his left lower abdomen, as if to perform tomoe-nage.

97. Your partner blocks the throw by stepping forward with his right foot, then tries to lift you up.

98. Shift your hips to the right, push on the inside of his left knee with your right foot, and pull him forward. Hook your left leg over his right and wedge your left foot against his right lower abdomen, then twist your hips to the right.

99. Straighten your left leg and pull with both hands to apply the lock.

Your partner attempts to escape by twisting to the left, then surrenders.

100. Release his arm. You both then sit up and face each other in the high kneeling posture.

101.

102.

103.

104.

105.

106.

At the conclusion of *ashi-garami*, take two steps back to the far position. Your partner takes one step back to his starting position. Face each other in the high kneeling position. (*Figs. 101–3*) Then both stand and take the basic natural posture. (*Fig. 104*) Take one step backward together with your right foot, kneel and bow to each other. (*Fig. 105*) Both of you then stand, turn to face the joseki, and finish with a standing bow. (*Fig. 106*)

14. Kime no Kata

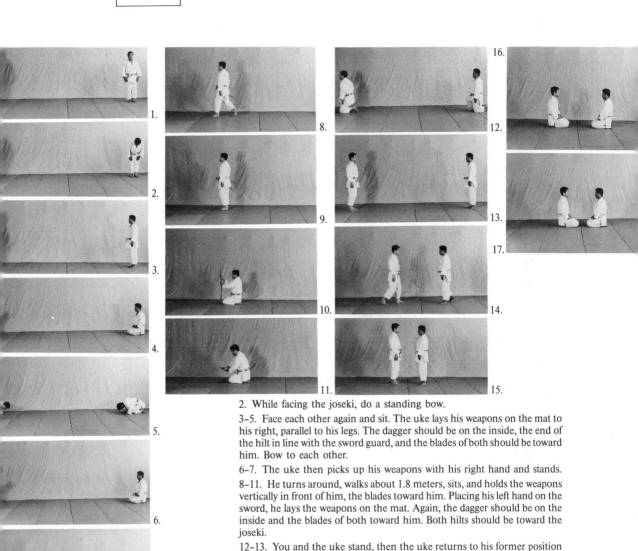

2. While facing the joseki, do a standing bow.

3–5. Face each other again and sit. The uke lays his weapons on the mat to his right, parallel to his legs. The dagger should be on the inside, the end of the hilt in line with the sword guard, and the blades of both should be toward him. Bow to each other.

6–7. The uke then picks up his weapons with his right hand and stands.

8–11. He turns around, walks about 1.8 meters, sits, and holds the weapons vertically in front of him, the blades toward him. Placing his left hand on the sword, he lays the weapons on the mat. Again, the dagger should be on the inside and the blades of both toward him. Both hilts should be toward the joseki.

12–13. You and the uke stand, then the uke returns to his former position facing you.

14–17. Take a step forward together, beginning with your left foot, and stand in the basic natural posture. Now move to within about 90 centimeters of each other, stop, and sit. Advance to within two fist-widths of each other (the *hiza-zume* position) by placing your fists on the mat and pulling yourselves forward.

The twenty techniques of Kime no Kata are given in Table III on p. 146.

To begin the kata, you and your partner stand facing each other about 5.4 meters apart. You are on the right as seen from the joseki. Your partner holds a sword and a dagger in his right hand, the sword on the outside, the blades of both upward. The tip of the dagger's hilt should be in line with the sword guard. (*Fig. 1*)

173

Ryote-dori   Two-Hand Hold

18.   19.   20.

21.
23.   22.
24.   25.

18. Place your hands naturally on your thighs, with your fingers pointing inward.

19. Your partner shouts, comes up on his toes, and grabs both your wrists, his thumbs on the inside.

20. Bring your knees together and pull your hands backward and out. While breaking your partner's balance to the front, raise your hips and come up on your toes.

21. Shout and kick him in the solar plexus with the ball of your right foot.

22. Bring your right knee back down and pull your left hand free. Take hold of his left wrist from below with your right hand, thumb on the inside, and turn to your left.

23-24. Raise your left knee, bring his left arm forward, and take the wrist from beneath with your left hand. Trap his left arm in your right armpit, and while pulling him forward, apply pressure to his elbow. This armlock is called *waki-gatame*.

25. Your partner pats you or the mat twice to indicate that he surrenders.

26.

27.

28.

29.

30.

31.

32.

33.

26. Return to the hiza-zume position and sit naturally.

27. Your partner raises his hips, comes up on his toes, shouts, and punches at your solar plexus with his right fist.

28. Dodge the punch by coming up on your toes, pivoting to the right on your left knee, and raising your right knee.

29. Grab his right sleeve with your left hand and pull the arm forward. At the same time, shout and punch him between the eyes with your right fist.

30. Immediately take his right wrist from the top with your right hand, thumb toward you, pull the arm to your right hip, and hold it against your thigh.

31. Reach around his neck with your left hand and grab high on his right lapel to apply a choke.

32. Apply an armlock (*hara-gatame*) to his right elbow by pushing against it with your lower abdomen.

33. Your partner surrenders by patting you or the mat twice.

Suri-age

34.	35.	36.	37.

34. Return to the hiza-zume position.

35. Your partner raises his hips, comes up on his toes, shouts, and thrusts the palm of his right hand at your forehead in an effort to push your head back.

36. Lean back a bit and turn slightly to your left while raising your hips and coming up on your toes. Deflect the blow by taking his right wrist from above with your right hand, your palm away from you.

37. Lay the palm of your left hand on his right shoulder and break his balance forward with both hands.

38. At the same time, kick him in the solar plexus with the ball of your right foot.

39. Immediately pivot to the right on your left knee and bring your right knee down to the mat. Pull him forward with both hands.

40. Twist him down onto his face. The palm of his right hand faces down. While pushing with your left hand and pulling with your right, take a step forward on your left knee, then your right.

41. Lower your hips and place your left knee on the back of his elbow. Apply an armlock by pulling up with your right hand.

Yoko-uchi   # Side Blow

42.	43.		45.

42. Return to hiza-zume.

43. Your partner raises his hips, comes up on his toes, shouts, and strikes at your left temple with his right fist.

44. Raise your arms and right knee and avoid the blow by ducking to his right side.

45. While coming up on your toes and stepping forward with your right foot, hold him as in kata-gatame.

46–47. Press your left hand against the back of his right hip and push him down to his right back corner.

48. Press against his right elbow with your left hand, come up on your knees, and raise your right hand, fingers together.

49. Strike him in the solar plexus with your right elbow.

    You and your partner then sit about 1.2 meters apart, facing each other.

46.	47.

48.	49.

Forehead Thrust

38. 39. 40. 41.

Ushiro-dori
Hold from Behind

50. 53. 56. 59.

51. 54. 57. 60.

52. 55. 58. 61.

50–52. Your partner stands and walks around behind you from your right side, stopping one pace directly to your rear.

53. He sits down and pulls himself forward until his knees are about 20 centimeters from your hips.

54. Next he raises his right knee and comes up on his toes, then leans his head a bit to the left, shouts, and puts his arms around your upper arms. You react by raising your arms to your sides.

55. Clasp his arms to you with your right hand, grab as high on his left sleeve as you can with your left hand, raise your hips, and come up on your toes.

56. Slide your right leg back between his legs.

57–58. Roll to your left as if performing seoi-nage.

59–60. While controlling him with your right arm in his right armpit, shout as you punch him in the groin with your left fist.

62. 63. 64. 65. 66.

Tsukkomi   # Dagger Thrust to Stomach

69. 70. 71. 72.

73. 74. 75. 76.

77. 78. 79. 81.

80. 82.

69–71. Your partner sits in front of the weapons and places the dagger, blade up, inside his jacket above the belt.

72–75. He then returns to his position in front of you, sits, and moves to the hiza-zume position.

76. Gripping the dagger scabbard from outside the jacket with his left hand, he unsheathes the dagger with his right.

77. Raising his hips and coming up on his toes, he steps forward with his left foot, shouts, and attempts to stab you in the solar plexus.

78. Pivot to your right on your left knee, come up on your toes, and raise your right knee. Deflect the

blow with your left arm and break his balance to the front.

79. At the same time, shout and punch him between the eyes with your right fist.

80. Immediately take his right wrist from above with your right hand, pull it to your right hip, and hold it against your right thigh.

81. Reach around his neck with your left hand and grip high on his right lapel. Apply a choke.

82. Simultaneously apply hara-gatame to his right arm by pushing your lower abdomen forward.

Return to the sitting position. You partner places the dagger back inside his jacket.

67. 68.

61-65. After completing ushiro-dori, your partner takes up his sitting position behind you, then stands and goes around your right side, stopping about 1.2 meters in front of you.

66-68. He then does a sitting bow, stands again, turns, and goes to get the dagger.

Kirikomi   ## Downward Slash

83.   84.   85.   86.

87.   88.
89.   90.

91.

92.

93.

83. Your partner reaches inside his jacket with his right hand and takes the sheathed dagger out, then transfers it to his left hand and holds it at his left side.

84. He unlocks the dagger with his left thumb and draws it out with his right hand.

85. Raising his hips and coming up on his toes, he takes a step forward with his right foot, shouts, and tries to slash the top of your head.

86. Pivot to the right on your left knee, come up on your toes, and step back with your right foot. At the same time, raise your arms and catch his right wrist in your right hand.

87. Put your left hand on top of his wrist.

88. Break his balance to the front.

89. Trap his right arm in your left armpit.

90. Twist to your right to apply waki-gatame.

91-93. After he surrenders, your partner returns to his original position, puts the dagger back into its scabbard, and places it inside his jacket.

Yoko-tsuki

94.

95.

96.

97.

94–96. Your partner stands, comes over to your right side, and sits next to you at a distance of about two fist-widths.

97. Gripping the dagger scabbard from outside the jacket with his left hand, he unsheathes the dagger with his right.

98. Coming up on his toes, he steps toward you with his left foot, shouts, and attempts to stab you in the right side. The blade is up.

99. Come up on the toes of your left foot, pivot 180 degrees to the right on your left knee, and raise your right knee. Deflect his arm at the elbow with the palm of your left hand and break his balance forward. At the same time, shout and punch him between the eyes with your right fist.

100–1. Immediately take his right wrist from above with your right hand, pull the arm to your right hip, and hold it against your right thigh.

102–4. Reach around his neck with your left hand and grab high on his right lapel. Apply a choke while applying hara-gatame to his right arm.

105.

106.

107.

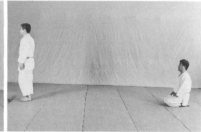

108.

109.

110.

105–7. You and your partner return to your starting positions next to each other. Your partner places the dagger back inside his jacket, stands, and sits down facing you about 90 centimeters away.

108–11. He then stands, turns around, and walks to where the sword is. He kneels and lays the dagger down in its original position.

111.

Dagger Thrust to Side

98. 99. 100. 101.

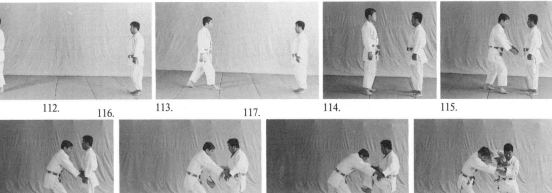

102. 103. 104.

Tachiai

Ryote-dori   ## Two-Hand Hold

112. 116. 113. 117. 114. 115.

118. 119.

112–14. Your partner and you stand, then he turns and comes to within about 90 centimeters of you.

115–16. He shouts, steps forward with his right foot, and takes hold of both your wrists.

117–18. Break his balance forward by pulling back and out with your arms, shout, and kick him in the groin with the ball of your right foot. Bring your right foot back down immediately.

119. Take his left wrist from underneath with your right hand, your thumb on the inside, and raise the arm. At the same time, pull your left hand free, turn and step to your left, and pull his left arm straight in front of you.

120–21. Put your left hand on the wrist, too, trap the arm in your right armpit, and apply waki-gatame.

120. 121.

122.

123.

124.

Sode-tori

122–25. Your partner walks behind you from your right side and stands to your left rear corner.

126. He grabs the middle of your left sleeve from behind with his left hand, then takes it with his right and lets go with his left. He twists and pushes the arm to force you to walk forward. Step forward with your right foot, then your left.

127. On the third step, step to your right front to break his balance in that direction.

128. Shout and kick him in the right knee with the side of your left foot.

129. Immediately place your left foot down near his right foot, and pivot 180 degrees to your left.

130–33. Take the inside middle of his right sleeve with your left hand and his left lapel with your right, and throw him with a right osoto-gari.

129.

Tsukkake   **Punch to Face**

134.

135.

136.

137.

138.

139.   140.

134. Stand and face each other at a distance of about 2.4 meters.

135. Your partner takes a big step forward with his left foot, raises his left fist to eye level, and holds his right fist at stomach level ready to punch you with his left hand.

136. Suddenly he lunges forward with his right foot, shouts, and tries to punch you between the eyes with his right fist.

137. Step to your left front corner with your left foot and turn to your right to avoid the blow. Take his right forearm from the top with your right hand and pull it forward and down, breaking his balance to the front.

138. As he tries to straighten up, step around behind him with your right foot, then your left.

139. Put your right arm around his throat and pull him backward.

140. Clasp your hands over his left shoulder as in hadaka-jime.

141. Draw your left foot back and apply the choke.

141.

Sleeve Grab

125.

126.

127.

128.

130.

131.

132.

133.

Tsukiage   Uppercut

142.

143.

144.

145.

146.

147.

148.

142. Stand facing each other about 90 centimeters apart.

143. Your partner steps forward with his right foot, shouts, and attempts to deliver a right uppercut to your chin.

144–45. Lean backward, take his wrist with both hands, and pull it upward.

146. Twist to your right.

147. Trap the arm in your left armpit.

148–149. Apply waki-gatame.

149.

Suri-age

150.

151.

152.

153.

Yoko-uchi   Side Blow

158.

159.

160.

161.

162.

163.   164.

158. Stand facing each other about 90 centimeters apart.

159. Your partner steps forward with his right foot, shouts, and tries to strike you on the left temple with his right fist.

160. Dodge the strike by bending forward and stepping in with your left foot. As you do so, take his left lapel in your right hand.

161. Step behind him with your right foot, then your left.

162. Reach around his neck with your left hand and grab the top of his right lapel.

163. Press your forehead against the back of his head, then pull him backward by stepping back with your left foot and lowering your hips, and apply okuri-eri-jime.

164–65. He attempts to defend himself by pulling down on your left elbow with both hands. Unable to escape the hold, he gives you the signal of defeat.

165.

Forehead Thrust

154.

155.

156.

157.

150. Stand facing each other about 90 centimeters apart.

151. Your partner steps forward with his right foot, shouts, and tries to strike you on the forehead with the palm of his right hand, fingers straight and together.

152. Lean back and parry the blow at the elbow with your left forearm.

153. At the same time, shout and punch him in the solar plexus with your right fist.

154-57. Immediately place your left foot in front of his left foot, bring your right foot back, and throw him with a left uki-goshi.

Keage

166.

167.
168.

169.

170.

171.

Groin Kick

172.

173.

166. Stand facing each other about 90 centimeters apart.

167-68. Your partner takes a small step forward with his left foot, shouts, and tries to kick you in the groin with the ball of his right foot.

169-70. Step back with your right foot and turn to the right. Catch his ankle from beneath with your left hand.

171. Place your right hand on the ankle and pull the leg to your left.

172-73. Twist your hips to the left, shout, and kick him in the groin with your right foot.

Ushiro-dori

174.

175.

176.

177.

181.

182.

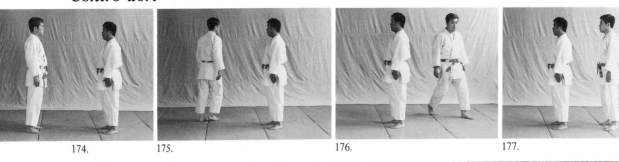

183.

174. Stand facing each other about 90 centimeters apart.

175–77. Your partner moves around behind you from your right side and stands about 75 centimeters directly in back of you.

178–79. Both of you take a step forward with your left feet, then your partner steps forward with his right foot and grabs you around your upper arms.

180–81. Immediately move your elbows outward and take his right upper sleeve with both hands.

182–83. Drop onto your right knee, your instep off the mat, and throw him with seoi-nage.

184–85. Shout and strike him between the eyes with the knife edge of your right hand.

186.

188.

187.

189.

190.

186–90. Stand together. Your partner goes to get the dagger as before, returns, and stands about 90 centimeters in front of you.

Hold from Behind

178.

179.

180.

184.

185.

Tsukkomi

Dagger Thrust to Stomach

191.

193.

195.

192.

194.

196.

197.

198.

191. Stand facing each other about 90 centimeters apart.

192. Your partner puts his left hand on the scabbard from outside his jacket and draws the dagger with his right hand. He steps forward with his left foot, shouts, and attempts to stab you in the stomach.

193. Move your right foot back, turn to the right, and deflect his right arm with your left hand on his elbow. Shout and punch him between the eyes with your right fist.

194. Immediately take his right wrist from above with your right hand and pull it toward your right hip.

195. Hold it against your right thigh, pulling him off balance.

196. Reach around his neck with your left hand, grab high on his right lapel, and step forward with your right foot, then your left.

197-98. Continue forward with your right foot, applying a choke and a hara-gatame armlock at the same time.

Kirikomi

199.   200.   201.

199. Face each other about 90 centimeters apart.

200. Your partner takes the dagger out of his jacket with his right hand and sticks it in his belt on the left side.

201. He then stands naturally again.

202. Next he unlocks the dagger with his left thumb and draws it with his right hand.

203. He steps forward with his right foot, shouts, and tries to slash you on the top of the head.

204. Lean back and catch his right wrist in both hands.

205. Move your right foot back a bit and turn to the right.

206. Bring your left foot in front of his right, pull him down to his right front corner, and trap his arm in your left armpit.

207. Apply waki-gatame.

208.   209.   210.

211.   212.   213.

214.   215.   216.

208-9. Face each other again. Your partner puts the dagger back in its sheath at his left side.

210. Then he places it back inside his jacket.

211-17. He turns and walks to where the sword is, sits and lays the dagger down in its original position, picks up the sword, and sticks it in his belt in the left side, cutting edge up. He then returns to stand about 1.5 meters in front of you.

217.

Downward Slash

202. 203. 204.

205. 206. 207.

Nuki-kake   ## Sword Unsheathing

218. 222. 219. 223. 224. 220. 225. 221. 226.

218. Your partner puts his right hand on the sword hilt.

219–20. He steps forward with his right foot and attempts to draw it.

221. Step close to his right foot with your right foot, and place your right hand on his right wrist from the top.

222. Immediately step to his rear with your right foot.

223. Bring your left foot around behind him and reach around his neck with your left hand, grabbing high on his right lapel.

224. Stick your right arm through his right armpit, palm up.

225. Bring your right hand up and place it on the back of his neck.

226. Step back with your left foot, breaking his balance to his left back corner, and apply kata-ha-jime.

227.

228.

229.

230.

231.

232.

233.

234.

235.

236.

227. Stand facing each other about 2.4 meters apart.

228. Your partner steps forward with his right foot and slowly draws the sword. He holds it with the tip level with your eyes (the *seigen* position).

229. He then advances a step by tsugi-ashi. Take a step backward, beginning with your left foot.

230. Your partner raises the sword high above his head while coming up on his toes (the *jodan* position).

231. He then shouts, steps forward with his right foot, and tries to slash you on the top of the head. Dodge the blow by stepping to your left front corner and turning to the right.

232. Lay your right hand on top of his right wrist.

233. Pull the wrist to your right hip and force him down toward his right front corner.

234. Reach around his neck with your left hand and grab high on his right lapel. While applying a choke, step forward with your right foot, then your left.

235–36. Take one more step forward with your right foot, and apply hara-gatame.

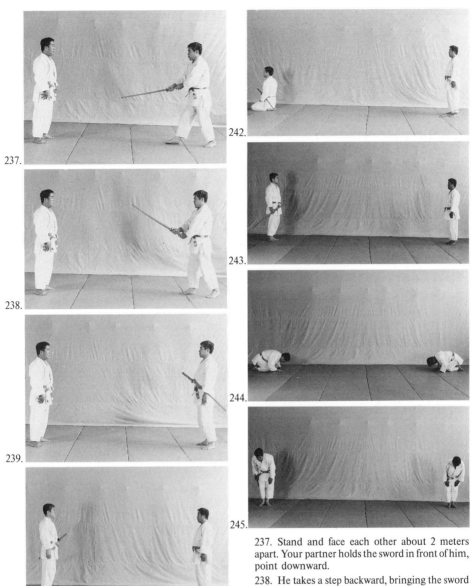

237.

238.

239.

240.

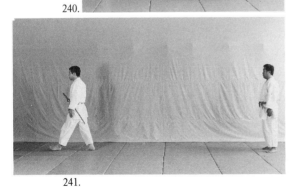

241.

242.

243.

244.

245.

237. Stand and face each other about 2 meters apart. Your partner holds the sword in front of him, point downward.

238. He takes a step backward, bringing the sword point up to eye level.

239–40. Then he returns the sword to its sheath, takes another step backward with his right foot, and stands naturally.

241–43. Your partner turns and goes to where the dagger is. He sits, removes the sword from his left hip, and returns it to its original position on the mat. Then he picks the sword and dagger up with his right hand, stands, and turns to face you.

244. Take a step backward together, sit, and bow to each other. Your partner lays the weapons on the mat to his right before he bows.

245. Your partner picks up the weapons, you both stand, turn toward the joseki, and do a standing bow.

15. Kodokan Goshin Jutsu

The Kodokan Goshin Jutsu is the newest kata, having been created in 1956. It complements Kime no Kata and is composed of a number of self-defense techniques making use of throws, armlocks, strikes and kicks. These actual combat forms include defenses against all forms of armed or unarmed attacks.

The twenty-one techniques incorporated in this kata are given in Table IV on p. 146.

1.   2.   3.   4.   5.   6.

1–3. Your opponent has a pistol inside his judogi and a stick and a dagger in his right hand. Both of you do standing bows, first toward the joseki and then to each other.

4–6. He kneels facing the joseki and places the weapons on the mat.

He returns to his original position and stands facing you. You advance toward each other and take the basic natural posture.

Ryote-dori   ## Two-Hand Hold

7.

8.

9.

10.

11.

12.

7. Your partner steps forward with his left foot and takes hold of both your wrists.

8. He attempts to kick you in the groin.

9. Step back with your left foot and free your right arm by jerking your fist toward your chest while pushing your elbow forward.

10. Strike your partner's right temple with the knife edge of your right hand.

11. Grab his right wrist from the top, step back with your right foot, and twist to the right.

12. Clamp his arm under your left arm and twist the wrist.

Hidari-eri-dori   ## Left-lapel Hold

13.

14.

17. 15.

18.

16.

13. Your partner grabs your left lapel with his right hand, steps forward with his right foot, and tries to push your down.

14. Grasp your own left lapel with your left hand and step back with your left foot. Strike at your partner's eyes with the back of your right hand.

15. Immediately grab his right wrist from the top with your right hand.

16. Put your left hand on his right elbow and step back with your right foot.

17. While twisting his wrist and pushing his elbow, bring him down on his face on the mat.

18. Put your left knee against the right side of his back and push his right arm toward his head.

Migi-eri-dori   **Right-lapel Hold**

19.   20.   21.   22.   23.

19. Your partner grabs your right lapel with his right hand, steps back with his left foot, and tries to pull you down.

20. Step forward with your right foot and deliver an uppercut with your right fist.

21. Grab his right wrist from the top with your left hand and press it firmly against your chest.

22. Step back with your left foot and turn your body slightly to the left.

23. Grab his right wrist with your right hand, fingers on the inside, and pull him forward until he falls.

Kataude-dori   **Single-Hand Hold**

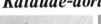

24.   25.   26.

28. 29.

27.

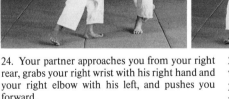

24. Your partner approaches you from your right rear, grabs your right wrist with his right hand and your right elbow with his left, and pushes you forward.

25. Step forward with your left foot to keep your balance.

26. Turn and kick the left side of his left knee with the sole of your right foot.

27. Put your right foot back down, step forward with your left, then withdraw your right.

28. Turn slightly to your right, grab his wrist from underneath, and hold it against your chest.

29. Twist to your right, clamp your left arm over his right arm, and press down on his elbow with your left armpit.

Ushiro-eri-dori

Collar Hold from Behind

30.

31.

32.

33.

34.

35.

30. Your partner approaches you from behind, grabs the back of your collar, steps back with his left foot, and tries to pull you down on your back.

31. Step back with your left foot.

32. Turn to your left on the ball of your left foot and raise your left arm to protect your head.

33. Punch your partner in the solar plexus.

34–35. Immediately apply a left ude-gatame to his right arm.

Ushiro-jime

Choke from Behind

36.

37.

40.

38.

41.

39.

36. Your partner puts his right arm over your right shoulder and attempts to apply hadaka-jime.

37. Tuck in your chin and pull his right arm down with both hands.

38. Lower your body, advance your right foot, and turn to the left.

39. Controlling his right arm with your right shoulder, slip your head free of his armpit and pull your left foot back behind his right.

40. Grip his right wrist from below with your left hand, fingers and thumb toward him, and press on his elbow from above with your left hand.

41. Step back again with your left foot, pull, and apply te-gatame to his right elbow to force him to the mat, face down.

Kakae-dori

42.

43.

44.

45.

AGAINST UNARMED ATTACK: AT A DISTANCE

Naname-uchi

48. Your partner raises his right arm and steps forward with his right foot, aiming a blow at the left side of your head.

49. Step outside his right foot with your left, turn to your right, and parry his right arm with your left.

50. Deliver an uppercut with your right fist.

51. Grab his throat with your right hand, your thumb to the left.

52–53. Take his right upper arm in your left hand and throw him with a right osoto-gari.

48.

49.

Ago-tsuki

54.

55.

56.

57.

Gammen-tsuki

60. Your partner steps forward with his left foot and punches at your face with his left fist.

61. Dodge the blow by stepping forward with your right foot, and punch him in the side with your right fist.

62–63. Move by tsugi-ashi to get behind him.

64–66. Apply hadaka-jime, stepping backward with your left foot, then your right.

60.

61.

Seize and Hold from Behind

46.   47.

42. Standing behind you, your partner steps forward with his right foot and puts his arms around you in a bear hug.

43. As soon as he touches you, stomp on his right foot with the ball of your right foot, step forward with your left foot, lower your hips, and free yourself by pushing your elbows forward.

44. Turn back, grasp his right wrist from the top with your left hand, and bring your right forearm up against his elbow.

45. Advance your left foot while controlling his wrist.

46. Step back with your right foot and turn to your right.

47. As you do so, throw your partner to your right back corner by twisting and pushing his right arm.

Slanting Strike

50.   51.   52.   53.

Uppercut

58.   59.

54. Your partner steps forward with his right foot and aims an uppercut at your chin.

55. Take a small step back with your left foot and deflect the blow from below with your right hand.

56. Grab his right wrist with your right hand and his elbow with your left hand, thumb down.

57. Twist the wrist away from you and push the elbow toward his face.

58–59. When his elbow locks, step forward with your left foot and throw him forward.

Thrust-Punch to Face

62.

63.

64. 65.   66.

Mae-geri   **Front Kick**

67.   68.   69.   70.

67. Your partner attempts to kick you in the groin with his right foot.

68. Dodge the kick by taking a step back with your right foot and turning to your right.

69. Grab his ankle with both hands.

70–72. Push him back until he falls on his back.

71.   72.

Yoko-geri   **Side Kick**

73.   74.   75.   78.

76.

77.

73. Your partner steps to his left front corner with his left foot, twists to the left, and tries to kick you in the right side with his right foot.

74–75. Step to your left front corner with your left foot, then your right foot, and parry the kick with your right forearm.

76. Continue to move forward until you are directly behind him. Put your hands on his shoulders.

77–78. Drop to your left knee and pull him down on his back to your right.

AGAINST ARMED ATTACK

Tsukkake   **Thrust**

79.

81.

83.

80.

82.

84.

79. Your partner steps back with his right foot, reaches inside the fold of his judogi with his right hand, and takes out a dagger, which he holds at his right side.

80. Before he can strike, step deeply in to his left side, take his left elbow in your right hand, thumb up, and hold your left hand in front of his eyes to blind him.

81. Grab his left wrist with your left hand and twist it away from you.

82. Twist your right hand to the left until your thumb is down, and push his elbow up.

83–84. Step back with your left foot and pull him down on his stomach by putting pressure on his elbow.

Choku-zuki   **Straight Thrust**

85.

86.

89. 87.

88.

90.

85. Your partner steps forward with his left foot, takes out a dagger with his right hand, then steps forward with his right foot and attempts to stab you in the stomach.

86. Step forward with your left foot, turn your body slightly to the right, and grab his right elbow from below with your left hand.

87. Deliver an uppercut with your right fist.

88. Take his wrist from below with your right hand.

89. Place your left hand on top of the wrist.

90. Break his balance to his right front corner, clamp your left arm over his right arm, and apply pressure to the elbow.

Naname-zuki   **Slanting Stab**

91.   92.   93.   94.

95.   96.   97.

91. Your partner steps forward with his left foot, takes out a dagger with his right hand, and raises it to strike. He steps forward with his right foot and attempts to stab you in the neck.

92. Avert the attack by stepping back with your right foot and turning to the right. At the same time, grab his right wrist from the top with your left hand.

93. Put your right hand on the bottom of his wrist.

94. Step back with your left foot and bring him down by twisting the arm and applying pressure to the wrist.

95–97. Apply te-gatame, and take the dagger away from him.

Furiage   **Upswing against Stick**

98.   99.   100.

101.   102.   103.

98. Your partner, holding a stick in his right hand, steps back with his right foot and raises the stick over his head.

99–100. Before he can strike, step in with your left foot, block his right arm with your left forearm, and push up on his chin with your right hand.

101-3. Throw him with right osoto-gari.

Furioroshi　　　　　　　　　　Downswing against Stick

104.

105.

106.

107.

108.

109.

104. Your partner, holding a stick, steps forward with his right foot, raises the stick to the side, and attempts to strike you on the left side of your head.

105. Avoid the blow by bringing your right foot back a bit.

106. Step forward with your left foot and hit him in the face with the side of your left fist.

107. Step behind his left foot and hit him in the face once again, this time with the knife edge of your left hand.

108-9. He falls on his back.

Morote-zuki　　　　　Two-Hand Thrust against Stick

110.

111.

112.

114. 115.

113.

110. Your partner is holding a stick in his hands. He steps forward with his left foot and attempts to hit you in the solar plexus.

111. Step forward with your right foot, turn your body to the left, and deflect the stick to your left with your right hand.

112. Grab the end of the stick from the top with your left hand.

113. Step forward with your right foot and grab the stick between your partner's two hands with your right hand.

114-15. Move forward, putting pressure against his left elbow with your right forearm, and throw him to his right front corner.

Shomen-zuke

116.   117.   118.

Koshi-gamae

Pistol Held at the Side

122.   123.

124.

122. Your partner steps forward with his left foot and holds a pistol at his side, pointing it at your abdomen. As you slowly raise your hands, he steps in close to you.

123. Twist to your left, grab the barrel from the top with your right hand and the bottom of the gun from below with your left hand.

124. Twist your hips to the right and pull in that direction with both hands. The pressure on your partner's wrist will force him to let go of the pistol.

125. Take it away from him and hit him on the head with it.

125.

Pistol at the Abdomen

119. 120. 121.

116. Your partner steps forward with his right foot and presses a pistol against your abdomen.

117. Raise your hands slowly, then twist to your right and step forward with your left foot. Grab the pistol with your left hand, thumb on top, and his right wrist from the top with your right hand.

118–21. Push the barrel of the gun toward his right armpit and disarm him.

Haimen-zuke Pistol against the Back

126. 127. 128. 129.

130. 131.

126. Your partner, with a pistol in his right hand, holds it against the middle of your back.

127. While slowly raising your hands, twist to your right.

128. Continue turning to your right and wrap your right arm around his right arm.

129–31. Take the gun away from him with your left hand.

At the completion of the final technique your partner puts the pistol back in his jacket and you stand face to face. Walking to the place where he left the dagger and stick, he kneels to pick them up in his right hand, carries them as at the beginning of the kata, and returns to stand before you. Each steps forward with his right foot, you bow to each other, then turn and bow in the direction of the joseki.

16. Ju no Kata

There are fifteen techniques arranged in three sets in the Ju no Kata. They are given in Table V on p. 147.

BEGINNING THE KATA

You, tori, and your partner, uke, stand facing each other about 5.4 meters apart. You are on the left as seen from the joseki. (*Fig. 1*) Turn and do a standing bow to the joseki, then face each other again and do a standing bow. (*Fig. 2*) Step forward at the same time with your left foot into the basic natural posture. Starting with your left foot, advance to within about 1.8 meters of each other and again take the basic natural posture. (*Fig. 3*)

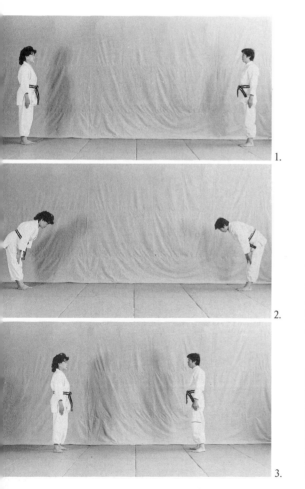

1.

2.

3.

SET 1

Tsukidashi

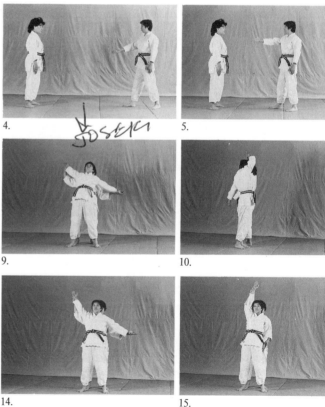

4.

5.

9.

10.

14.

15.

4–5. Your partner moves forward by *tsugi-ashi*, her right foot leading. As she moves, she raises her right arm straight out in front of her, the extended fingers held together.

6. As she nears you she aims her hand at the point between your eyes.

7. Dodge the blow by turning your face to the right, then step back with your right foot and turn 180 degrees to the right. Take her right wrist from the bottom with your right hand, your knuckles toward you, and pull her forward.

8. When her body is directly in front of you, take her left wrist with your left hand, your thumb on top. Extend her right arm diagonally up and the left arm diagonally down.

9. Lean backward, pulling her with you.

10. In an effort to free her right hand, your partner drops her right shoulder and twists to the left, pulling back her left foot.

11. She then grabs your wrists and turns all the way around. Meanwhile you have turned around to face in the opposite direction.

12. She steps slightly forward with her right foot, raising your left arm slightly and lowering your right arm, and leans back, pulling you against her chest.

13. This time you twist to the right, pulling your right foot back, and take hold of her wrists. Continue turning until she stands in front of you.

14. Move your left foot forward, raise her right arm up and lower her left arm. Lean back pulling her against your chest.

15. Lower her left arm directly downward with your left hand and raise her right arm with your right.

16. Slide your left hand up to her shoulder.

17–18. Move back, beginning with your right foot, and break her balance to the rear.

Your partner pats her leg once with her left hand to signal defeat. Return her to the basic natural posture. In each of the following techniques as well, the uke surrenders by patting once with her hand or stomping once with her foot, at which point you return her to the basic natural posture.

Hand Thrust

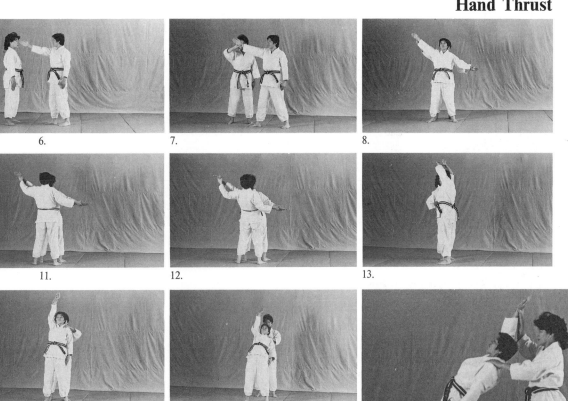

6.

7.

8.

11.

12.

13.

16.

17.

18.

19.

20. JOSEKI

21.

22.

23.

24.

25.

27.

28.

26.

19. You and your partner face in the same direction, the joseki on your left. Your partner stands at your left back corner, her right foot in line with your left. She raises her extended right arm to shoulder height.

20. Placing her right hand on your left shoulder, she pushes you forward. You bend at the hips.

21–22. She bends forward too. (*Fig. 22* is side view.)

23–24. Bend as far forward as you can, then gradually move backward, starting with your right foot.

When her hand slips off your shoulder, grab it with your right hand. Take two or three more steps back while maintaining your balance. (*Fig. 24* is side view.)

25. Your partner pivots to her right on her right heel, then steps forward with her left foot and tries to strike you between the eyes with her extended left fingertips.

26–28. Move backward and grab her left hand with your left hand. Pull both her hands up and bend her backward.

29.   30.   31.   32.

33.   34.   35.

36.   37.

29. Stand facing your partner about 45 centimeters apart. You are on the left as viewed from the joseki. She grabs both your wrists.

30–32. Pull your hands back to break her balance to the front, then turn to the left and take her right wrist with your left hand from underneath. Free your right hand by pulling it to your left shoulder. (*Fig. 32* is back view.)

33. Step to your left front corner with your right foot and extend your right arm across her right arm.

34–35. While pivoting to the left on your right foot, grab her arm at the elbow with your right hand and trap it in your right armpit, then lower your hips and pull her against your back. (*Fig. 35* is side view.)

36–37. Lift her up by straightening your legs and bending forward.

38. Your partner stands directly behind you. The joseki is to your left.

39. Your partner brings her hands up to her shoulders.

40. She places them on your shoulders.

41. Pulling with her left hand and pushing with her right, she turns you to your left.

42. Pivot on your left foot so that you face her, and put your left hand on her right upper arm, near the shoulder.

43-44. Slide the hand down her arm and grab inside the elbow, then step back with your left foot and break her balance to the front.

45-46. Step forward with your right foot, drop your hips, and bring your left foot back near the inside of her left foot. Put your right shoulder in her right armpit, lay your right hand on her right shoulder, and left her as in ippon-seoi-nage.

47.

48.

49.

50.

51.

52.

53.

54.

55.

47. Start with your partner standing behind you with the joseki on your left. Then step forward with your right foot, then your left, pivot to the right on your right foot, and stand in the basic natural posture.

48. Beginning with her right foot, your partner moves forward by tsugi-ashi, raising her right arm, fingers extended straight, as she goes.

49. She tries to push the right side of your jaw with her right hand.

50–51. Turn your left foot, your body and your face to the left. Grab the palm of her right hand with your right hand, and break her balance to the front. (*Fig. 51* is back view.)

52. Swing your right foot forward, then pivot on it 180 degrees to your left, ducking under her right arm and attempting to twist it.

53. Your partner steps forward with her left foot and tries to strike you between the eyes with the fingers of her left hand. Lower your hips and catch her left hand from the bottom with your left hand.

54. Step back with your right foot, then your left, and pull her arms up and back. She swings her right foot around behind her and leans back.

55. When her arms are fully extended, bring her hands down to her shoulders and break her balance to the rear.

SET 2

Kirioroshi

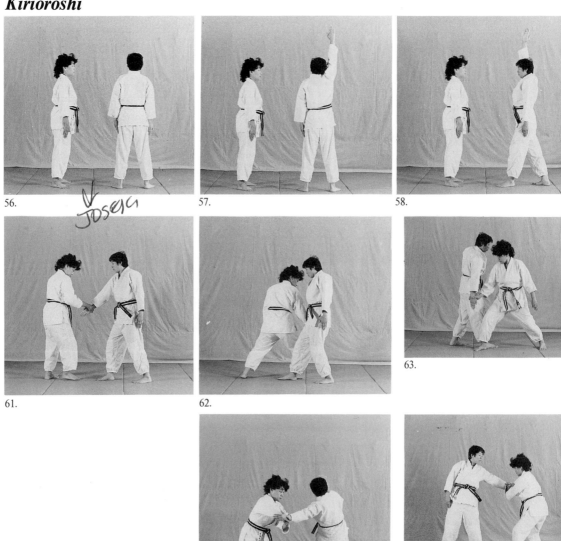

56.

JOSEKI

57.

58.

61.

62.

63.

67.

68.

56. You and your partner face each other about 90 centimeters apart. Your partner draws her right foot back and turns to the right so that her back is to the joseki.

57. She raises her right hand above her head, the fingers straight and together.

58. Keeping her feet in place, she twists to the left to face you again.

59. She takes a big step forward with her right foot

and attempts to strike the top of your head with the knife edge of her right hand.

60. Avoid the blow by pulling in your jaw, bending back, and stepping back with your right foot, then your left.

61. When her right hand is at stomach level, take the wrist with your right hand and begin advancing with tsugi-ashi, your right foot leading.

62–63. Pull the arm straight and push it to her

59.

60.

64.

65.

66.

69.

70.

71.

right back corner to break her balance in that direction. (*Fig. 63* is back view.)

64. She draws her right foot back, turns to the right, places her left hand on your right elbow, and pushes you around to your left.

65–66. Let go of her right wrist, pivot to the left on your left foot, and extend your right arm upward. (*Fig. 66* is back riew.)

67–68. Turn completely around, step to her rear

with your right foot, and take her left hand with your left hand. Break her balance to her left rear corner. (*Fig. 68* is back view.)

69. Step behind her with your left foot, then your right.

70–71. Put your right hand on her left shoulder, turn your body to the left, and raise her left arm up and back. Take a big step back with your left foot and assume the defensive posture.

72. Your partner stands about 45 centimeters in back of you. The joseki is to your left. She raises her hands to her shoulders.

73. Then she raises them above her head.

74. She lowers her arms and places her hands on your shoulders, pushing down.

75–76. Bend your knees, lower your hips, pull your left foot back and begin pivoting to the left.

77. Turn around to face her.

78. Take her right wrist from below with your left hand and pull her forward.

79. Bring your left foot back behind your right and continue to pull her forward. She comes forward with her right foot.

80. Continue pivoting to the left and put your right hand on her wrist. When you are facing in the same direction as she, change your left-hand grip, holding with your thumb on the little-finger side of her wrist.

81. Move forward with small steps and straighten up. Bring her right arm up and forward with both hands in an effort to load her onto your back.

82. She resists by pushing against your left hip with her left hand.

83. Step to your right and twist your hips to the left while continuing to pull her forward with your right hand. Step behind her with your left foot and assume the defensive posture, Extend your left arm across her chest, and break her balance to the rear.

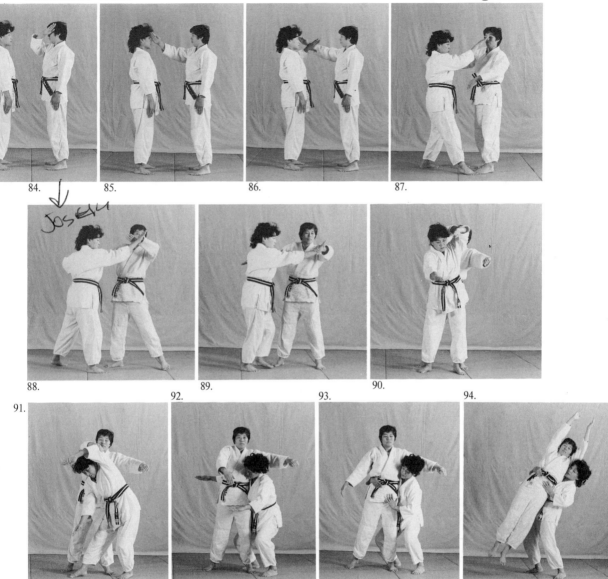

84. Stand facing each other about 45 centimeters apart. You are on the left as viewed from the joseki. Your partner brings her right hand up to the left side of her face.

85. She attempts to strike you between the eyes with the knife edge of her hand.

86. Avoid the blow by leaning back, and take her right wrist from the inside with the fingers of your right hand.

87–88. She steps back with her left foot, turns to the left, and grabs your right wrist with her left hand. Pulling it in the direction of the strike, she breaks your balance forward.

89. Step forward with your left foot, take her left wrist with your left hand, and try to break her balance to her left front corner. Free your right hand.

90. She then places her right hand on your left elbow and pushes it, causing you to turn your back to her.

91. Drop your hips, pivot to the right on your left foot, and bring your right foot back behind her.

92. Put your right arm around her waist.

93. Grab the front of her belt with your right hand and place your left hand on her lower abdomen as in ura-nage.

94. Straighten your legs, lean back, and pick your partner up. She holds her legs together and raises her arms straight above her head.

Katate-dori   **One-Hand Hold**

95.   96.   97.   100.   98.   101.

99.

95. Stand next to your partner facing the joseki. You are on her left.

96. Your partner takes your right wrist from the top with her left hand.

97. Step forward with your right foot, causing her to bring her right foot forward too, and raise your right arm, palm down, elbow slightly bent. Free the arm by pushing it toward your left front corner.

98. She then lays her right hand on your right elbow, passing her hand under her left arm, and pushes your upper body to your left.

99. Take her left arm with your right hand, slip your left arm around her waist, drop your hips, and load her onto your back as in o-goshi.

100. Straighten your legs and bend forward to raise her.

101. Your partner points her toes and arches her back.

Katate-age   **One-Hand Lift**

102. Stand facing your partner about 2.4 meters apart. You are on the left as viewed from the joseki.

103. Raise your right arms together, palms forward, and come up on your toes.

104. Approach each other with small steps. Just before you collide, step back with your right foot, turn to your right, and put your left hand on your partner's left shoulder. At the same time, she steps forward with her right foot and lowers her right arm.

105. Take her right arm at the elbow and bend her body to your right.

106. She then straightens up. As she does so, push up on her right elbow with your right hand. Let your left hand slip down to her left upper arm. Bend her to the left.

107. Again she tries to straighten up. Help her, and the moment she is upright, break her balance to the rear.

108–9. Slide your left hand back up to her left shoulder and your right hand up to her right wrist. Take a step back, beginning with your right foot, and in a defensive posture break her balance further to the rear by pulling her right arm up.

106.

102.
107.

103.
108.

104.
105.
109.

110. 111. 112. 113.

114. 115. 116. 117.

118. 119. 120. 122. 123.

121.

110. Stand facing your partner about 60 centimeters apart. You are on the left as viewed from the joseki.

111. Your partner takes a small step forward with her left foot, crosses her hands, left on top, raises them, and tries to take hold of your belt from the front.

112–13. Move your hips back slightly, take her left wrist from below with your right hand, and pull it toward your left. (*Fig. 113* is back view.)

114–15. Reach over your right arm with your left hand and take her left elbow from beneath. Turn her around to her right. (*Fig. 115* is back view.)

116–17. When her back is to you, place your right hand on her right shoulder and continue turning her to her right. (*Fig. 117* is back view.)

118–19. As she comes around to face you again, she takes your right elbow from below with her right hand and turns you around to your left. (*Fig. 119* is back view.)

120. When your back is to her, she places her left hand on your left shoulder and attempts to turn you around to face her.

121. Before she can do so, put your left arm around her waist, take her left arm with your right hand, and bend your knees as in o-goshi.

122. Load her onto your hips.

123. Pick her up as in katate-dori.

124.   125.   126.   127.

128.   129.   130.

132.   133.

131.

124. Stand facing each other about 25 centimeters apart, you on the left as viewed from the joseki.

125. Your partner raises her right hand and pushes against the left side of your chest. Lean back a bit, then bring your left hand up, catch her right wrist between your thumb and fingers, and push the hand up.

126. Push the right side of her chest with your right hand.

127. She leans back and pushes your right hand up with her left. Let your left hand drop to your side naturally. She takes your left wrist with her right hand.

128. She pulls your left wrist diagonally down to your left while extending your right arm up to your right.

129. Pull your left hand down in front of your body, lower your left shoulder, and step to your right with your left foot, pulling your right shoulder back. Take her left wrist with your right hand. Your partner, meanwhile, lowers her right shoulder and begins to turn to her left.

130. Turn together until you stand back to back. Your left arm is up, your right arm down.

131. Continue turning in the same direction until you face each other. Take her left wrist with your right hand and lift it diagonally to the right. Take her right wrist with your left hand and pull it diagonally down to your left. Break her balance to the rear.

132. Let your right hand slip down to her left elbow and step behind her with your right foot.

133. Bring her right wrist to your left hip, lower your hips somewhat, and break her balance further to the rear.

134.

135.

136.

137.

138.

139.

140.

141.

142.

143.

144.

145.

134. Stand facing your partner about 75 centimeters apart, you on the left as viewed from the joseki.

135. Your partner steps back with her right foot and raises her right arm, her hand open and the palm away from her.

136. She swings the arm down behind her and clenches her fist at her hip.

137. Then she steps forward with her right foot and aims an uppercut at your chin.

138. Pull in your chin, lean your upper body back, and catch her fist with your right hand.

139. At the same time, put your left hand on her right elbow, step forward with your left foot, and turn her to her left.

140. She pivots 180 degrees on her left foot and faces you again.

141. Take her right elbow with your left hand.

142. Pull your left foot back and push the arm up, causing her to step forward with her right foot.

143. Move forward a bit with your left foot and push against her elbow with your right hand to break her balance to the rear, then step behind her with your right foot.

144–45. Extend your right arm back over her right shoulder and and grab your left upper arm, trapping her right arm in ude-garami. (*Fig. 145* is back view.)

Uchioroshi

146.

147.

148.

149.

150.

151.

153.

154.

155.

156.

157.

Ryogan-tsuki

161. Stand facing your partner about 75 centimeters apart. You are on the left.

162. Your partner raises her right hand to chest level, her fingers extended and separated at the middle and ring fingers.

163. Stepping forward with her right foot, she tries to hit your eyes with her middle and ring fingers. Step back with your left foot, turn to the left, and take her right wrist with your left hand. Pull the arm forward and down.

164–65. She brings her left foot forward, takes your left wrist with her left hand, and pushes it, freeing her right hand. She then tries to force you down to your left rear.

166–67. Push on her left elbow with your right hand. She bends her knees and pivots around to the right on her right foot, ducking under your right arm.

168. Step forward with your left foot and strike at her eyes with the fingers of your left hand. She steps back with her right foot, turns to the right, takes your left wrist from the inside with her right hand, and tries to pull you forward and down.

169. Step in front of her with your right foot, grab her right wrist with your right hand, and push to free your left hand. Start to pull her forward with your right hand. She pushes on your right elbow with her left hand.

170. Without moving your feet turn your upper body to the left.

171. Take her left upper arm with your right hand, put your left arm around her waist, drop your hips, and pull her to you as in ogoshi.

172. As she is lifted, she straightens her legs and arches her back.

161.

162.

163.

168.

169.

170.

171.

172.

Downward Strike

146. Stand facing each other at a distance of about 75 centimeters. You are on the left as seen from the joseki.

147-48. Your partner spreads the fingers of her right hand and brings it across to her left, then up above her head in a circular movement.

149. She brings the arm back down in the same clockwise movement while clenching her fist, and then brings the fist up in front of her face.

150. Then she raises the fist above her head.

151. Stepping forward with her right foot, she tries to strike the top of your head with the side of her fist. Take a step back, beginning with your right foot, and bend your body back to avoid the blow.

152. Her fist passes in front of your face.

153. When the fist comes down to the level of your abdomen, grab the wrist with your right hand. Move forward with your right foot by tsugi-ashi.

154. Push her right arm back to break her balance to her right rear corner.

155-56. She draws her right foot back and turns to her right, puts her left hand on your right elbow, and turns you to your left.

157. Pivoting on your left foot, step behind her with your right foot so that you stand at a right angle to her. Take her left wrist with your left hand, and break her balance to the rear.

158. Step around behind her.

159. Put your right arm around her neck.

160. While choking her with your right arm, step back with your left foot, bring her left wrist to your left hip, and apply an armlock.

152.

158. 159.

160.

Strike to Both Eyes

164. 165. 166. 167.

173. 174. 175.

After executing the last technique, return to your starting positions, one step in front of your initial bow. (*Fig. 173*) From the basic natural posture, take one step backward with your right foot. Bring your feet together. (*Fig. 174*) Do a standing bow to each other (*Fig. 175*), turn to face the joseki, and do a standing bow.

17. Itsutsu no Kata

FORM 1

1. 2.

6. 7. 8.

1-2. Stand facing your partner at a distance of about 3.5 meters. You, the tori, should be on the right as seen from the joseki. Turn and bow to the joseki, then bow to each other.

3-6. Slowly approach your partner with ayumi-ashi, starting with your left foot, raising your right palm as you go. Continue forward on a slight angle to your left until your right foot almost touches his, then place your palm gently on his chest, your thumb out to the side.

7-8. Take a step forward with your left foot and push him back with the thumb side of your right

FORM 2

12. 13. 14. 15.

The five forms in Itsutsu no Kata are identified only by number. (Professor Kano died before giving them names.) They are meant not only to demonstrate the principle of maximum efficiency, but also to be evocative of the movements of the universe.

On completion of Form 5, you return to your original positions, bow to each other and in the direction of the joseki.

3.

4.

5.

9.

10.

11.

hand so that he takes a small step back with his left foot. Now step forward with your right foot and push with the little-finger side of your hand. He should step back on his right foot.

9. Continue advancing with small steps, pushing alternately with the thumb side and the little-finger side of your hand, gradually increasing your pace. Unable to keep up with you, your partner finally loses his balance. At that point, step forward with your right foot and push hard with your right arm.

10–11. He falls straight back, slaps with both hands, then immediately sits up, legs apart.

16.

17.

18.

12–14. Your partner slowly raises his right knee and holds his right hand at his waist with the fingers pointing straight ahead. Then he stands, and lunges forward on his right foot as if to stab you with his right hand.

15. Step back with your left foot, turn your body to the left, and grab his right wrist with your left hand, thumb on the bottom. Place your right hand on the inside of his forearm and pull him off balance to his right front corner.

16. As you pull, drop to your left knee and throw him with uki otoshi.

17. He falls in an arc past your left side and lands on his back.

18. He slowly sits up.

FORM 3

19. 20. 21. 22.

25. 26. 27. 28. 29.

FORM 4

31.

32.

33.

34.

35.
36.

37.

38.

39.

40.

41.

This form is meant to represent the movement of the tide as it flows in and out, sweeping away things on the shore.

31. Slowly stand and turn to face your partner, who has his back to you. Step back with your left foot and turn your body to the left.

32-33. Swing your arms back to your left as if casting a net and bend forward a bit, then run toward your partner and let your arms swing forward.

34. Run just past him and stop with your right foot in front of his left.

35-36. Having raised your arms high to the front, spread them out to your sides. Lower your left arm slowly and hold it at the left side of your belt. At the same time, bring your right arm down to shoulder level, then step back enough to bring the arm into contact with your partner's chest. Now take a step back with your right foot and push him back with your arm.

37. Your partner takes several small steps back in an effort to regain his balance.

38. Stepping back yourself, keep up the pressure on his chest, then drop to your left knee.

39-41. He falls back like a log.

23. 24.

30.

19-20. Your partner rises to his left knee, then you and he stand while raising your arms to your sides.

21-24. Circle around each other to the left in smaller and smaller circles, like Chinese phoenixes.

25. When you reach the center you should meet face to face. Let your arms cross, left arms on top.

26-29. Continue rotating to your left, picking up speed, then slip your feet past your partner's right foot and drop on your back. As you fall, pull down in an arc with your left hand and push up and over with your right. Your partner flies over your body.

30. After he lands on the mat he rises to his feet, while you lie spread-eagled.

FORM 5

42. 43. 44.

45. 49. 50. 46. 51. 47. 52. 53. 48.

42. Stand in opposite corners with your backs to each other.

43. You and your partner then step forward with your right feet and raise your arms to your sides like Chinese phoenixes.

44-46. Pivot on your left feet until you are face to face and then run toward each other.

47-50. Just before you collide, throw your legs forward in front of your partner's legs and drop to your side.

51-53. He flips over you, does a forward roll, and stands.

18. Koshiki no Kata

OMOTE

Tai

1. 2. 3.

7. 8. 9.

13. 14. 15.

The techniques in this kata were designed for armor-clad warriors of the Kito School, and it is essential while performing the kata to imagine oneself wearing heavy armor. I decided to preserve the techniques in the form of this kata because of the extent to which they embody the principle and techniques of Kodokan judo.

The kata is divided into the two parts, *omote* (front) and *ura* (back), and twenty-one techniques given in Table VI on p. 147.

As with the other kata, Koshiki no Kata begins with you and your partner facing each other (about 5.4 meters apart). Turning toward the joseki, perform a standing bow. (*Figs. 1–2*) This is followed by a sitting bow. When ending the kata, the sitting bow is done first and is followed by a standing bow.

4.　　5.　　6.

10.　　11.　　12.

16.　　17.　　18.　　19.

5-7. You turn and face the joseki, and after calming your mind and body through deep abdominal breathing, take a step forward on your left foot and stand ready.

8-10. Beginning with his left foot, your partner walks forward until his right foot is in front of your left foot, then he stops and takes the front of your belt in his left hand and the rear in his right.

11-12. He swings his left leg up and back down, using the momentum to draw you close to his right hip, and attempts to apply a hip throw.

13-15. Put your left hand against the back of his

hips and your right hand on the left side of his chest, and break his balance to the rear.

16-17. Drop to your right knee and throw him to your left back corner.

18-19. After falling, your partner sits up, spreads his legs a bit, and places his hands on his thighs. Meanwhile, you put your left hand on your left knee, rise on the ball of your right foot, and move your left leg out to your left.

After a few seconds, the two of you rise slowly to your feet and return to your original positions.

Yume-no-uchi

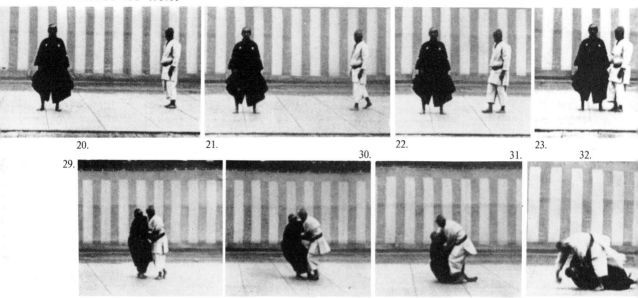

20.   21.   22.   23.   32.

29.   30.   31.

20-27. Your partner approaches you and attempts a hip throw as in the last technique.

28. Again you try to break his balance to the rear, but he resists you by stiffening his body.

29. Lift him with your left hand, which is at the rear of his waist, turn to face him, and lightly grab his left upper inner sleeve or his chest with your right hand.

30. Lean back and take several small steps to your rear to break his balance.

31. When he is tilted forward and his weight is on his toes, throw yourself backward.

32-35. Your partner rolls forward and comes to his feet facing you. You remain on your back for a few seconds, with your arms and legs spread.

Ryokuhi   Strength Dodging

36.   37.   38.   39.   40.

36. You and your partner face each other at a distance of about 90 centimeters.

37-39. Your partner steps forward with his left foot, then his right, and with his arms crossed, right arm on top, tries to take hold of your belt with both hands.

40. Step back with your right foot and draw your hips back. Your partner loses his balance to the front.

41. Turn your body to your right and take his right wrist in your left hand, thumb on top. Reach over your left forearm with your right hand and place it on his right elbow. Control his right arm with both your hands. While leading him to the right with your right hand, move your left hand to his left upper arm, near the shoulder, and push him until he is close to your right front corner. Off balance to the front, he straightens up. Place your right hand on his right shoulder and your left hand on his left upper chest, drop to your left knee, and pull your right hand backward and downward.

42. He falls directly back.

41.   42.

Dreaming

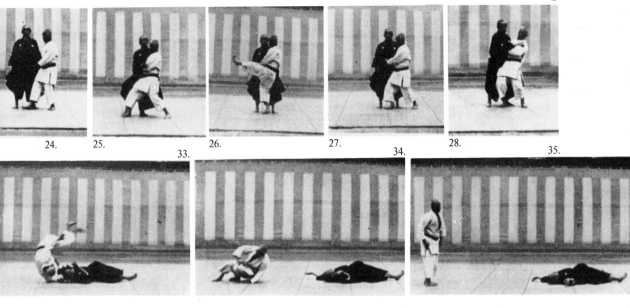

24.   25.   26.   27.   28.

33.

34.   35.

Mizu-guruma   # Water Wheel

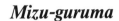

43.   44.   45.   47.

43. You and your partner stand about 1.8 meters apart.

44. As in the last technique, he attempts to grab your belt with both hands, one over the other. Step back with your right foot, take his right wrist in your right hand, thumb on the bottom, and grab his right upper arm with your left hand.

45. Pull the arm down.

46. He resists by straightening up.

47. As he does so, push his right forearm up to his forehead with your right hand and put your left hand on the small of his back. Break his balance to the rear.

48. He now bends forward to regain his balance.

49–53. As he does so, fall back and throw him over you as in yume-no-uchi.

48.   49.   50.

51. 52.   53.

Mizu-nagare   **Water Flow**

54.

55.

56.

59. 60.

57.

58.

54. You and your partner stand about 3.5 meters apart. You are on the right.

55. Begin walking toward each other.

56. When you are about 1.8 meters apart, your partner goes through the motions of unsheathing with his right hand an imaginary dagger worn on his right hip. Stepping forward with his left foot, he grabs for your lapels with his left hand.

57. Before he can touch you, take a small step back with your right foot and lean back a bit. As he stretches to reach you, he loses his balance to the front. Grab his left wrist with your right hand, thumb on top, and the inside of his left elbow with your left hand. Gently pull him forward.

58–59. Take a big step back with your right foot, drop to your right knee, and throw him to his left front corner by pulling with both hands.

60. He lands on his back, then sits up, spreads his legs, and places his hands on his thighs.

Hikiotoshi   **Draw Drop**

61.

62.

63.

64.

67.

65.

66.

61. Stand on the left, about 1.5 meters from your partner.

62–63. He steps forward with his left foot then his right and tries to twist you from left to right by pushing your left shoulder back with his right hand while pushing up on your right shoulder with his left hand.

64. Turn your body to the left, grab his right forearm with your left hand, and place your right hand on his right upper arm near the shoulder.

65–67. Drop to your left knee and throw him by pulling him to his right front corner with both hands. As in the last technique, he sits up after he falls.

Ko-daore   Log Fall

68.   69.   70.   71.

72.   73.   74.

68. Stand on the right, about 2.7 meters from your partner.

69-70. Move toward each other, raising your right arm, held with the fingers straight as if it were a sword. When about 1.8 meters from your partner, step forward with your right foot and thrust your right hand at his forehead.

71. He evades you by stepping back with his right foot and turning his face to the right, and takes your right wrist in his right hand.

72. He turns and pulls you to the right, puts his left arm around your waist, and attempts to apply a left hip throw.

73-74. Stretch your right arm out and bring it back against his forehead, breaking his balance to the rear. Step close to him with your right foot, grab the front of his belt with your left hand, and pull him to you. He resists by pulling back. Break his balance to the rear and throw him by dropping on your left knee. Your partner sits up after his fall, while you come up on the ball of your left foot and move your right knee out to the right.

Uchikudaki   Smashing

75.   76.   77.   78.

79.   80.   81.   82.

75-76. Stand on the left and approach your partner as in ko-daore, raise your left hand, and thrust it at his abdomen.

77. He turns to his left, grasps your left wrist in his left hand, and draws you to the left. Stepping in front of you with his right foot and putting his right arm around your waist, he tries to execute a right hip throw.

78. Break his balance to his left back corner by pressing your left arm against his chest and pushing against the front of his belt with your right hand.

79-80. As he steps back to recover his balance, move with him and drop to your right knee.

81-82. He falls directly back, then sits up. You come up on the ball of your right foot and move your left knee to the left.

Tani-otoshi   Valley Drop

83.   84.   85.   86.   87.
   89.   90.   91.
88.

83. You and your partner face the joseki, he about 1.8 meters behind you to your left rear.

84–85. He comes up to your left back corner, puts his right hand on the back of your right shoulder and his left hand on the front of your belt, and tries to push you down to the front.

86–87. Bend forward as far as you are pushed so that his right hand slips off your shoulder, then grab the fingers of his right hand with your right hand and pull down to the front.

88. He steps in front of you with his right foot and straightens up in an effort to regain his balance.

89. Straighten up and place your left foot behind his right foot, then trap his body between your left leg and your left arm. Bring your left hip up behind his right hip, put your right hand on the right front side of his belt, and break his balance to his left back corner.

90–91. Drop to your right knee and throw him to his left back corner. Finish as in the previous technique.

Kuruma-daore   Wheel Throw

92.   93.   94.   95.
   97.   98.   99.
96.

92–94. Your partner again approaches you from the left rear and tries to twist you down by pushing forward and downward on your right shoulder with his right hand while pushing back against your left shoulder with his left hand.

95. Without resisting, pivot on your left foot and bring your right foot around until you face him.

96. Move your left foot to the left, grab his left upper arm near the armpit with your right hand, and slip your left hand through his right armpit, placing it on the back of his right shoulder.

97. Pull him to the front with both hands and throw yourself backward.

98–99. Your partner flies directly over your head.
   He stands after he falls, while you remain motionless for a few seconds.

Shikoro-dori   Grabbing the Neckplates

100.   101.   104.   102.   105.   106.

103.

100. Stand on the right, about 90 centimeters from your partner.

101. He steps forward with his left foot and tries to grab the front of your belt with his left hand.

102. Evade his grasp by moving your hips back, take his left wrist in your right hand, and pull it to your left. At the same time, twist his jaw away from you with your left hand.

103. His right foot comes off the ground and he loses his balance to his rear.

104-5. Move your right hand to his right shoulder, drop to your left knee, and pull him hard to his right back corner with your right hand.

106. He sits up and you kneel as usual after the throw.

Note: Originally the throw was effected by twisting an opponent's neckplates.

Shikoro-gaeshi   Twisting the Neckplates

107.   108.   111.   109.   112.   113.

110.

107. As in the last technique, stand on the right, about 90 centimeters from your partner.

108. He steps forward with his left foot, grabs the front of your belt from the top with his left hand, pivots on his left foot, and tries to throw you with a left hip throw.

109. Step forward with your right foot, yielding to his pull.

110. Push the left side of his head with your right hand and pull his jaw toward you with your left hand, breaking his balance to his right.

111. He tries to right himself.

112. Throw him by sitting down and pulling his right shoulder directly downward with your right hand.

113. Your partner sits up after his fall and you remain sitting.

Yudachi **Shower**

114.   115.   116.

117.  118.  119.

114. Stand on the left this time, about 90 centimeters from your partner.

115. Reach forward with both hands and bring his lapels together, then grip them with your right hand, the index finger inserted between the lapels and bent inward at the second joint. Your partner steps forward with his left foot and takes the bottom of your right middle sleeve in his left hand.

116. Step back with your right foot. He then steps forward with his right foot, puts his right arm around your waist, and tries to throw you with a right hip throw.

117. When he brings his body close to you, step back with your left foot, turn to your left, and grab his right arm with your left hand.

118. Drop to your left knee and pull him down to his right back corner with both hands.

119. He sits up after his fall and you kneel.

Taki-otoshi **Waterfall Drop**

120.   121.   122.   123.   124.

126.   127.   128.

125.

120. Stand on the right and, as in the previous technique, grab your partner's lapels with your right hand, the index finger inside.

121. He steps forward with his left foot and grabs your right middle sleeve from underneath with his left hand.

122. Step back with your right foot.

123. He steps forward with his right foot, puts his right arm around your shoulder, and tries to execute a right hip throw.

124. Put your left hand on his waist and break his balance to the rear with your right hand, which is still holding his lapels.

125. He resists by leaning forward. Break his balance to the front as in yume-no-uchi and throw yourself backward.

126–28. He rolls and stands, while you lie spread-eagled for a few seconds.

Mi-kudaki   **Body Smashing**

129.

130.

131.

132.

133.

134.

135.

136.

137.

138.

139.

129. Stand on the left, facing the joseki. Your partner stands on the right, facing you, about 2.7 meters away.

130–33. As in tai, he walks up to you, grabs both sides of your belt, swings his left leg up and then down, and tries to apply a right hip throw.

134. Grab his left wrist with your right hand, put your left arm under his left armpit, and break his balance to his rear by moving to your left.

135. He resists by leaning forward.

136–38. Step to his right side with your right foot then your left, and throw yourself backward.

139. Your partner lands well past your head.

Kuruma-gaeshi   **Wheel Throw**

140.   141.   142.   143.

140. Your partner immediately stands and rushes at you to push you backward.

141–43. Just before his hands meet your shoulders, put your hands on his upper arms from underneath, step in past his right foot with both your feet, and throw yourself backward.

Mizu-iri   **Water Plunge**

144.   145.   146.   147.

149.   150.

148.

144–45. Your partner stands and rushes at you again, this time attempting to push your left shoulder with his right hand.

146–50. Grab his right with your left hand, place your right hand underneath his right upper arm, slip your feet to his right side, and throw him over you.

Ryusetsu   **Willow Snow**

151.   152.   153.   154.

151. As your partner stands, run toward him. When about 90 centimeters away, hold your right arm out with the wrist bent down and quickly flip your hand up so that the palm faces him. (This sort of feint is known as *kasumi*, literally, "mist.") He averts his face to his right. Step into his right side.

He looks forward again. Take hold of his left lapel with your right hand, put your left hand through his right armpit and place your hand on the back of his right shoulder.

152–54. Break his balance to the front, fall back, and throw him over you.

Sakaotoshi   **Headlong Fall**

155.   156.   157.

159.

160.

158.

155. As soon as he stands up, your partner approaches you and tries to stab you in the stomach with his left hand, as if it were a dagger.

156. Step back with your right foot, turn to your right, grab his left wrist from above with your right hand, and put your left hand on the inner side of his left upper arm.

157. Pull him hard to his left front corner.

158–60. Just as he is about to fall on his face, he turns and lands on his back.

Yukiore   **Snowbreak**

161.   162.   163.

164.

165.   166.

161. Stand and walk forward. Your partner stands and comes after you.

162. He starts to put his arms around your shoulders.

163–66. Before he has a chance to lock his arms around you, grab his right arm with both hands, drop to your right knee, and throw him with seoinage.

Iwa-nami   **Wave on the Rocks**

167. 168.   169.   170.   171.

172.   173.   174.   175.

167. Your partner stands and comes toward you.

168. When he is about 90 centimeters away, feint with both hands to make him turn his face to his right.

169–70. As he looks forward again, take his left lapel in your right hand and his right lapel in your left, slip your feet past his right foot, and throw yourself back. Pull hard with both hands as you fall.

171–73. Your partner flies over your head, then stands after his fall.

174–75. Return to your starting positions, bow to each other, then bow to the joseki.

V
HEALTH AND FIRST AID

19. Seiryoku Zen'yo Kokumin Taiiku

As discussed in chapter 2, a system of physical education ideally possesses three characteristics: it promotes the development of strong, healthy minds and bodies, is interesting, and is useful. Not only does Seiryoku Zen'yo Kokumin Taiiku meet all three requirements admirably, it goes well beyond being merely gymnastics or simply a martial art.

This kata consists of two groups of exercises. One is practiced alone, the other with a partner. All but one of the exercises have direct applications in self-defense.

Being able to perform martial arts techniques requires good muscular development. It is well to remember that physical well being does not appear as if by magic after a week or a month of training. We know from experience that beginning students listen attentively to fundamental instructions, hoping to progress quickly to advanced combat forms. This is a mistake. The foundation must be laid first and the superstructure built by degrees. There is even danger in undertaking advanced training before the preliminaries have been mastered. For those who take the steps in sequence and train properly, the rewards are perfect physical development and proficiency in techniques.

Maximum-Efficiency National Physical Education has been designed to appeal to the public of all ages. Practicing the movements is an ideal way to warm up before doing randori or practicing kata and to warm down after practice. By doing so regularly, one strengthens muscles, providing more power to apply to judo techniques and greatly reducing the risk of injury during randori. For this reason, I have long recommended the kata, particularly to beginners, to women and to children under fifteen. Like mastering falls, it is a fundamental part of judo training, which no beginning judoka can afford to overlook.

In the Individual Exercises, there are strikes directed against an imaginary assailant. This is a unique kind of training because the muscles have to both execute the strike and stop it, there being no actual target. Sufficient practice will produce muscles that react swiftly and are graceful to look at, like the musculature seen in ancient Greek athletes. Interestingly, they contrasted with the later Roman athletes, whose muscles tended to be round and chunky.

Tandoku Renshu　　　INDIVIDUAL EXERCISES

Each of these exercises should be performed powerfully and with maximum speed at the moment of impact. Unless performed as if you were actually attacking an enemy, they will lack spirit. When striking with the fist, your arm should make contact with the surface of your target at a right angle to it.

The explanations that follow are of right-handed forms. Do right- and left-handed forms of each exercise at least five times each. Whenever appropriate, return to the natural stance before starting the next exercise or series.

Goho-ate　　　　　　　　　　　　　　　Five-direction Strike

Hidari-mae-naname-ate　　　　　Left-front Crossing Blow

1.　　　　　　　　　　　　2.　　　　　　　　　　　　3.

1. Start in the basic natural posture.

2. Clench your right fist and draw it back to your side, the back of your hand to the right.

3. Punch to your left front corner and fix your eyes on your fist. Your right arm should be level with your shoulder. Draw your left arm back a bit.

Migi-ate　　**Right Side Blow**　　*Ushiro-ate*　　**Rear Strike**

4.　　　　　　　　　　　　5.　6.　　　　　　　　　　　　7.

4. Bring your right fist to the front of your left shoulder, with the back of the hand up.

5. Strike to your right with the side of your fist, then fix your eyes on the fist. Again your arm should be at shoulder level.

6. Put your right arm out in front of you. Open the hand and turn your palm up.

7. Immediately strike to your rear with your elbow. Be sure the elbow passes close to your side.

Mae-ate Front Blow

8.

8. Turn the palm of your right hand down and clench your fist. Punch to the front and fix your eyes on your fist. Your arm should be at shoulder level, with the back of your hand up.

Ue-ate   Upward Blow

9.   10.

9. Draw your right fist back to your right chest.

10. Tilt your head upward to the right and punch directly up, keeping your eyes on your fist. The back of your fist should be to the right. Bring your fist back down to your shoulder, then down to your side. Unclench your fist.

Ogoho-ate   Large Five-direction Strike

This group differs from Goho-ate in that (except for the last exercise) you take a step in the direction you strike in.

11.

Ohidari-mae-naname-ate
Large Left-front Crossing Blow

11. Step to your left front corner with your right foot and punch as in hidari mae naname ate.

Oushiro-ate
Large Rear Strike

14.

14. Drop your right arm to your side and unclench your fist. Step back with your right foot and strike to your rear with your right elbow.

Omigi-ate   Large Right Side Blow

12.

13.

12. Bring your fist back to your left shoulder.

13. Step back to your original position with your right foot and strike to your right.

Omae-ate   **Large Front Blow**

15. Step forward with your right foot and punch to your front.

16. Bring your right foot back to its original position and position your right fist at the level of your right shoulder.

17. Bend your knees a little. Jump up or rise to your tiptoes and punch straight up.

15.

Oue-ate   **Large Upward Blow**

16.   17.

Goho-geri   **Five-direction Kick**

Effectiveness in kicking depends directly on stability of the body as a whole. Keep your hips firm and steady.

Mae-geri   **Front Kick**

18.

18. Shift your weight to your left foot, bend your right knee slightly, draw the toes of your right foot back, and kick with the ball of your right foot at your opponent's kneecap. Keep your eyes on your toes.

Ushiro-geri   **Rear Kick**

19.

20.

21.

19–20. Bring your right foot up to your thigh and raise the leg until the thigh is horizontal.

21. Kick straight back at your opponent's kneecap or shin with your heel. Be sure you kick with the bottom of your heel, not the area near the Achilles' tendon.

Hidari-mae-naname-geri

Left-front Crossing Kick

22. Bending your right leg, raise the foot to your right back corner.

23. Kick with the ball of your foot to the kneecap of an opponent standing at your left front corner. Look at your toes.

22.

23.

Migi-mae-naname-geri

Right-front Crossing Kick

24. Bring your right foot across to the outside of your left leg.

25. Kick with the ball of your foot to the kneecap of an opponent standing at your right front corner.

24.

25.

Taka-geri

High Front Kick

26. Bring your right foot back.

27. Kick with the ball of your foot to the midsection of an opponent standing in front of you. Fix your eyes on your toes.

Note: To put power into your kicks, you must keep your hips steady.

26.

27.

Kagami-migaki   **Mirror Polishing**

This is the only symbolic exercise in this kata. It is performed as if one were polishing a large mirror. The mirror represents the human mind, the act of polishing the ethics by which our minds are refined. To go with this kata, I wrote a song, "Life is fighting to see justice done. . . . The most formidable enemy blocking the path to righteousness lies unseen within our hearts: evil thoughts. To rid yourself of evil, always polish the mirror in a serious frame of mind." Whether against enemies seen or unseen, execute every technique with true fighting spirit.

28.   29.   30.   31.

28. Spread your elbows to your sides and bring your hands in front of your chest, palms out, fingers spread apart.

29. Raise your hands in front of your face, at first letting your fingers overlap, right fingers in front of left.

30. Move your hands in opposite circles, up, out, and down, then back up. Let the fingers of your left hand come in front of those of your right as you bring your hands up to your face. Repeat the polishing movement several times.

31. Now polish in the opposite direction, down, out, up, and back down, again alternating the hand whose fingers go before those of the other hand.

Note: Move your hands in the same plane.

Sayu-uchi **Strike to Both Sides**

32. Clench your fists and bring your forearms to your chest, palms down, right arm on top.

33. Strike to both sides at once with your fists.

Relax your arms and bring them across your chest again, left arm on top. Strike again. After doing several sets, lower your arms and stand in the basic natural posture.

32.   33.

Zengo-tsuki   **Front-Rear Strikes**

34. Clench your fists and draw them back to your chest, palms down.

35. Punch with both hands at once to the front, keeping your eyes on your fists. Your arms should be at shoulder level.

36–37. Open your hands, turn the palms up, and strike to your rear with both elbows.

Repeat the exercise several times, then lower your arms.

34.   35.   36.   37.

38.   39.

Ryote-ue-tsuki Two-Hand Upward Blow

38. Clench your fists and raise them to your chest, palms inward.

39. Look up and punch straight up with both hands at once.
    Repeat the exercise several times.

Oryote-ue-tsuki Large Two-Hand Upward Blow

40.   41.

40–41. Go through the same motions as in the previous exercise, but jump up or rise on your tiptoes as you punch.

Ryote-shita-tsuki Two-Hand Downward Blow

44.   45.

44. Raise both fists to your armpits.

45. Raise your heels, bend your knees, and punch directly downward with both fists at the same time.
    Stand and repeat the exercise several times, then return to the natural posture.

Sayu-kogo-shita-tsuki Left-Right Downward Blows

42.  43.

42. Bring your right fist up to your armpit as though lifting a bag.

43. Bend to your right and punch down while drawing your left fist up into your left armpit. Keep your eyes on your right fist. The back of your right hand should face to your right.
    Repeat the movements to your left. Do several sets, then lower your arms.

Naname-ue-uchi Front-Side Upward Cut

46. Bring your right hand up to your left shoulder, palm down, thumb and fingers straight and held together.

47. With the knife edge of your right hand, strike the right temple of an opponent standing to your right front corner who is taller then you. Fix your eyes on the hand.
    Lower your right hand and go through the movements with your left hand. Do several sets, then take the natural posture.

Note: With this and the next technique, take special care to put snap into your strike.

46.  47.

Naname-shita-uchi

48.   49.

Front-Side Downward Cut

48. Raise your right hand to your left shoulder as in the previous exercise.

49. Strike with the knife edge of your hand at your opponent's wrist, which is at your right front corner. Keep your eyes on your hand. Lower your right hand and go through the movements with your left hand. After several sets, return to the natural posture.

Onaname-ue-uchi

50.   51.   52.

Large Slanting Upward Cut

50. Raise your right hand to your left shoulder as in the previous two exercises.

51. Stretch to your right, coming up on your left toes, and strike with the knife edge of your right hand at an opponent who is above you.

52. Alternatively, bring your right hand to your upper left chest, twist as far to your right as possible, letting your left arm come forward, and strike at an opponent directly behind you.

Repeat the exercise with your left hand and do several sets, then return to the natural posture.

Ushiro-sumi-tsuki

53. Bring your right fist above your shoulder, your elbow out to the right.

54. Pivot as far to the left as you can on the ball of your right foot while leaving your left leg where it is.

55. Punch down to your left rear with your right fist.

Repeat the exercise with your left hand and do several sets. Return to the natural posture afterward.

Rear-corner Blow

53.   54.   55.

Ushiro-uchi

56–57. Moving your right arm clockwise in a large circle in front of you, bring it up as if to wipe your brow with the back of your wrist, then punch down to your right rear.

58. As you punch, twist your body and neck as far to the right as you can. Fix your eyes on the fist.

Repeat the movements with your left arm and do several sets, then assume the natural posture.

Rear Blow

56.   57.   58.

Ushiro-tsuki/mae-shita-tsuki

59.   60.   61.

Rear/Downward Blows

59. Bend both arms and bring the fists up in front of your shoulders, the backs of the hands facing forward. Bend backward and punch over your shoulders at an opponent standing behind you. Your fists, the backs of the hands upward, should pass close to your ears.

60. Spread your elbows to the sides and return to an upright position.

61. Bend forward and punch straight down, the backs of your fists facing forward.
   Repeat the movement several times, then return to the natural posture.

Sotai Renshu   JOINT EXERCISES

This group of exercises is composed of *Kime Shiki* (Forms of Decision) and *Ju Shiki* (Forms of Gentleness). Within the Kime Shiki are idori (kneeling movements) and tachiai (standing movements).

When you finish all the Sotai Renshu techniques, repeat them (except for *gyakute-dori*) on the left side. Then sit and bow to your partner as you did before beginning Tandoku Renshu.

Kime Shiki   Forms of Decision

IDORI   Kneeling Techniques

Ryote-dori   Two-Hand Hold

62.   63.   66.   64.   67.   68.

65.

62. Sit and bow to your partner at a distance of about 1.8 meters. You, the tori, should be on the left.

63. Clench your fists and move forward together, using your arms like crutches, until your knees are 10 to 12 centimeters apart, then place your fists on your thighs.

64. Your partner grabs both your wrists, thumbs on the inside.

65. Pull your hands back to your sides and come up on your toes.

66. Move your left knee out to the left.

67-68. Step to the outside of your partner's right knee with your right foot and free your right hand by pushing it toward your left shoulder.
   Sit back down and put your fists on your thighs.

Furihanashi   # Shaking Loose

69.   70.

69. Repeat the movements of the last technique, but after freeing your right hand, put your right foot between your partner's knees and attempt to hit her between the eyes with the knife edge of your right hand. She blocks the blow by grabbing your wrist with her left hand.

70. Step way back with your right foot and whip your right hand to your right. Be sure to press the little-finger side of your wrist against the area between your partner's thumb and index finger and pry your wrist free as you pull.

Gyakute-dori   # Reverse Two-Hand Hold

71. Your partner grabs both your wrists, her thumbs on the outside.

72. Raise your right knee, placing it against her stomach, and come up on your left toes. Pull your hands directly backward.

73. Alternatively, you may clap your hands together behind your back after pulling them loose.

71.   72.   73.

Tsukkake   # Stomach Punch

74.   75.   76.

77.   78.

74–75. Your partner thrusts her right hand at your stomach. Raise your right knee and move your right foot back, twisting to your right. Deflect the blow by pushing her right elbow with your left hand.

76. Take her right wrist in your right hand and place it on your right thigh. Stick your left arm across her chest.

77–78. Press down on her elbow with your abdomen until she acknowledges defeat by patting her body with her free hand.

Kiri-gake   Head Cut

79.   80.   81.   82.   84.   85.

83.

79. Your partner goes through the motions of unlocking a short sword at her left side by pressing on its guard with the thumb of her left hand.

80–81. She then raises her right knee, unsheathes the sword with her right hand, and tries to cut you on the head. As she does so, you raise your right knee and step back with your right foot, twisting to your right. Deflect the blow by pushing her right elbow with your left hand.

82–83. Grab her right wrist from underneath with your right hand and trap the arm in your left armpit. Put your left hand on her wrist from beneath, too.

84–85. Push down against her elbow with your body. If necessary, twist the arm away from you. Release her when she signals defeat.

TACHIAI   Standing Techniques

Tsuki-age   Uppercut

86. Stand and face your partner. You should be about 60 centimeters apart.

87. She steps forward with her right foot and aims an uppercut at your jaw with her right hand. Step back with your right foot,

turn your hips to the right, and take her right forearm in your left hand.

88. Twist back to your left and punch her in the stomach with your right fist.

86.   87.   88.

Yoko-uchi   Side Blow

89. Stand about 60 centimeters from your partner.

90. She draws her right fist back and swings at your left temple while stepping forward with her right foot. Quickly step back with your right foot, drop your hips, and turn them to the right.

91. At the same time, deflect the blow with your left hand. Straighten up and bring your right fist to your hip.

92. Twist your hips back to the left and punch her between the eyes.

89.

92.

Ushiro-dori   Hold from Behind

93.   94.   95.

93. Your partner stands about 60 centimeters behind you. Stepping outside your right foot with her right foot, she begins to put her arms around you, placing the right side of her head against the left side of your neck to prevent you from butting her in the forehead.

94. Before she can tighten her grip, drop your hips, spread your arms to the sides, and step to your left back corner with your left foot.

95. Strike her in the stomach with your right elbow, stepping back with your right foot if necessary. Be sure to put snap into your blow.

Naname-tsuki   Carotid Cut

96.   97.   98.   99.

101.   102.   103.   104.

100.

96. Your partner stands about 60 centimeters in front of you, concealing a dagger in her right hand.

97-98. She steps forward with her right foot and tries to slash your windpipe from the left.

99. Evade the attack by stepping back with your right foot, turning to the right and dropping your hips. Deflect her right arm with your left hand.

100. Press the arm down with your left hand, then punch her hard between the eyes with your right hand while twisting to your left. Step forward with your left foot if necessary.

101-3. Step behind her and apply a half Nelson with your right arm.

104. Place the palm of your left hand on her chest near the left shoulder, and while pulling her to you with your left hand, push her head forward with your right, putting pressure on her right shoulder. Release her when she gives up.

Kirioroshi   **Downward Cut**

105.   106.

107.   108.

109.   110.   111.

105. Your partner stands about 1.8 meters in front of you with a sword (blade up) at her left side. She unlocks it by pressing on the guard with her left thumb.

106. Stepping back with her left foot and turning to the left, she draws the sword with her right hand and points it between your eyes.

107. Next she brings her left foot up even with her right and places her left hand on the end of the sword hilt.

108. Stepping back with her right foot, she raises the sword over her head.

109. Then she steps forward with her right foot and aims a blow at your head. Quickly step to the her left, turn to your right, and place your left hand on her forearm.

110. Grab her right wrist from above with your right hand and bring it tight against your right thigh. Stick your left arm across her chest.

111. Press down on her right elbow with your abdomen until she surrenders.

When you finish all the Sotai Renshu techniques, repeat them on the left side except for gyakute-dori, then sit and bow to your partner as you did before beginning Tandoku Renshu.

Ju Shiki   **Forms of Gentleness**

This group of exercises is made up of ten techniques from the Ju no Kata. Each is performed as in the kata. The starting distance is about 2 meters apart. The exercises are divided into two sets:

Set 1
Tsuki-dashi, kata-oshi, kata-mawashi, kiri-oroshi, katate-dori.

Set 2
Katate-age, obi-tori, mune-oshi, tsuki-age, ryogan-tsuki.

20. Kappo

Sasoi-katsu   **Inductive Method**

1-2. The patient should be sitting before you, one leg crossed. Bend your right knee and place the kneecap against his spine, letting your right heel come up off the mat. Spread your fingers and place your hands on his lower chest, hooking your fingers under his lower ribs. Pull back as if opening the ribs to either side, put your weight on the shoulders to bend his body back, and press forward with your right knee, letting your heel come down on the mat. This will draw air into his lungs. When his ribs have been opened as far as they will go, release them. Air will be exhaled from his lungs. Repeat the process slowly and regularly, at a rate of 10 to 15 times a minute, until he begins breathing by himself. If you see a slight effort to breathe on his part, take care to reinforce his movements, not to oppose them.

During practice and tournament competition, a judoka is sometimes choked into unconsciousness, and his breathing stops. He may be suffocated by congestion, anemia, brain compression or defective oxidation in the bloodstream caused by pressure on the carotid arteries, trachea or vagus nerves. If *kappo* (resuscitation techniques) are applied promptly, there is no cause for alarm.

Kappo developed as a part of jujutsu in the eighteenth century alongside *sappo*, the art of attacking the body's vital points. Both were treated as secret arts. Instruction was oral, and students were forbidden to pass their knowledge on to others without their master's permission.

Numerous methods of kappo have been devised, including *tanden-katsu* (lower abdomen method), *jinzo-katsu* (kidney method), *dekishi* or *sushi-katsu* (treatment for drowning victims) and *ishi-katsu* (handing treatment). The four techniques given below are the ones most often resorted to.

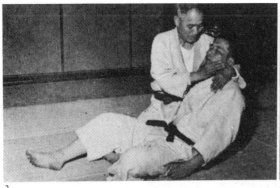

3.

4.

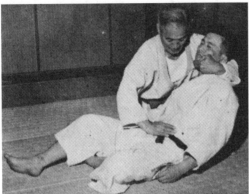

5.

6.

3. Kneel to the right of the patient and support his upper body with your left arm around his shoulder.

4. Put the palm of your right hand on his abdomen, just above the navel, and press up against the solar plexus or pit of the stomach. This will cause the diaphragm to rise, expelling air from the lungs.

5. Reinforce the action by bending his upper body forward with your left arm.

6. Gently release your pressure to allow air to enter the lungs. Repeat this procedure until respiration is restored.

If you want to administer medication, first open the patient's jaw with your right hand while holding your left hand on his forehead, and have someone else put it in his mouth. Then close his mouth, hold it shut with your left hand, and apply *eri-katsu*.

Before applying any of the resuscitation techniques, it is important to make sure that nothing obstructs the passage of air into the victim's lungs—for instance, food, water, the tongue, or some other object. Food or other objects can be removed with the fingers. Have someone hold the tongue for you if necessary, or tie a rubber band around it and loop the end around his chin. If you have a safety pin, you can pin his tongue to his judogi.

In the case of a drowning victim, you should first drain the water from his lungs by laying him face down, his head lower than his feet, and press against his lower back. Then roll him over and apply the first *so-katsu*. Ideally, a cylinder of some kind is rolled over the abdomen and chest. The victim should be kept as warm as possible.

A person knocked unconscious by a throw should be put to bed at once, with his feet elevated, and be kept warm. Avoid giving him medication, and send for a doctor at once.

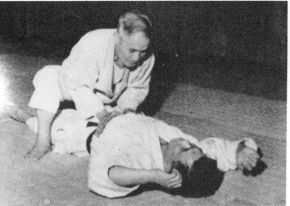

7.

8.

7. Lay the patient on his back and kneel astride him. Place your hands, fingers spread apart and pointing toward his head, on the bottom of his rib cage. Lean forward and press against his ribs to make him exhale, then relax the pressure. Repeat this procedure, rocking forward and back, until he can breath by himself.

8. A variation of this method is called the *jinzo-katsu* (kidney method). The patient is laid face down and upward pressure is applied against the waist or kidneys.

Kogan-katsu   **Testicle Method**

9.

10.

Also called the *inno katsu* (scrotum method), this is not a means of resuscitation but a treatment for a man whose testicles have been kicked up into his pelvis, either by a carelessly applied throw such as uchi mata, ouchi-gari or tomoe-nage, or by a kick.

9. Put your arms under the patient's armpits from behind and clasp your hands together.

10. Lift him up a bit and then let him drop. Repeat as necessary.

11. Alternatively, lightly kick him in the lower back with the ball of your foot.

11.

Appendix A: Jigoro Kano Chronology

1860   Born in Mikage, Hyogo Prefecture, on Otober 28. The third son of Jirosaku Mareshiba Kano, he was given the childhood name Shinnosuke.

1871   Entered Seitatsu Shojuku, a private school in Tokyo, where he received instruction from Keido Ubukata.

1873   Entered Ikuei Gijuku, a private school in Karasumori, Shiba, Tokyo. Received special instruction in English and German from native teachers.

1874   Entered Tokyo School of Foreign Languages.

1875   Entered Kaisei School.

1877   Entered Tenshin Shin'yo School and studied under Hachinosuke Fukuda. Received instruction in jujutsu for the first time.

1881   Graduated from Tokyo Imperial University, majoring in literature, politics and political economy.

1882   Became a lecturer and later a professor at Gakushuin. Founded the Kodokan.

1883   Founded the Kobunkan, a school for Chinese students, and became its principal.

1886   Appointed vice principal of Gakushuin.

1889   Resigned as vice principal of Gakushuin to accept a post in the Imperial Household Department. Made a study tour of educational institutions in Europe.

1891   Became principal of the Fifth Higher School in Kumamoto Prefecture.

1893   Became principal of the First Higher School in Tokyo, subsequently principal of Tokyo Higher Normal School.

1897   Resigned as principal of Tokyo Higher Normal School but later accepted the post again.

1901   Became principal of Tokyo Higher Normal School for the third time. By this time judo and kendo had come to enjoy great popularity.

1908   The Diet unanimously approved a bill requiring all middle schools to provide instruction in *gekiken* swordsmanship and jujutsu.

1909   Became the first Japanese member of the International Olympic Committee.

1922   Elected to the House of Peers.

1928   Attended the Olympic Games in Amsterdam as a member of the International Olympic Committee.

1938   Attended the International Olympic Committee meeting in Cairo, where he proposed that Tokyo be the site of the 12th Olympic Games. Died on May 4 at sea on the return voyage.

Appendix B: Guide to the Kodokan

LOCATION

The Kodokan, formally named the Kodokan International Judo Center, is located at the Kasuga intersection in Bunkyo Ward, and the address is 16–30 Kasuga 1-chome, Bunkyo-ku, Tokyo 112. The telephone number is (03) 3811-7151. The new eight-story ferroconcrete building was completed in March, 1984.

The Kodokan is convenient to public transportation. It is a short walk from the Japan National Railways' Suidobashi Station (Sobu Line), from Korakuen Station on the Marunouchi subway line and from Kasuga Station on the Mita subway line. A number of buses stop in front of the Bunkyo Ward Office, just around the corner.

New Building	Main Building
8F	
7F	7F
6F	6F
5F	5F
4F	4F
3F	3F
2F	2F
1F	1F
B	B

New Building

B Restaurant （食堂）

1F Entrance （入口）
Parking （駐車場）

2F Library （図書館）
Archives（資料館）
Kano Memorial Hall（嘉納師範室）
Judo Hall of Fame （柔道殿堂）
Research Center （科学研究室）
Exhibition Room （資料展示室）
Conference Room （会議室）
Classroom （教室）

3F Lodging Rooms （宿泊室）

4F Changing Rooms （更衣室）
Entrance to Dojo （道場入口）

5F Women's Dojo（女子部道場）
Boy's Dojo （少年部道場）
Special Dojo （特別道場）

6F School Dojo （学校道場）
International Division Dojo （国際部道場）

7F Main Dojo （大道場）

8F Spectator Seats （大道場見学席）

Main Building

B Training Room（トレーニング室）

1F Statue of Master Jigoro Kano（嘉納治五郎師範銅像）
Accounting Section（会計課）
Dojo Management Office（道場管理室）
Members Club（柔道人クラブ）
International Affairs Division（国際部）

2F Bldg. Maintenance（用務室）
Equipment & Supplies（振興課）
Service & Duty Management（業務課）
Promotion Committee Office（審議会調査部）
Editorial Office（編集部）
All Japan Judo Federation（全日本柔道連盟）
Judo Section, High School Athletic Federation（高等学校体育連盟・柔道）
Judo Section, Junior High School Athletic Federation（中学校体育連盟・柔道）
Tokyo Judo Federation（東京都柔道連盟）
All Japan Junior Judo Club Federation（柔道少年団）

3F President's Office（館長室）
Conference Room（会議室）
Advisors Room（参与室）

4F General Affairs（庶務課）
Judo Union of Asia（アジア柔道連盟）

5F Research Dojo（研究道場）

6F All Japan University Judo Federation（全日本大学柔道連盟）

ENROLLMENT

Anyone of any nationality may join the Kodokan. To apply for membership, it is only necessary to fill out an application form and present it, together with the application fee, to the Accounting Department. The applicant will be issued a certificate of membership and a magnetically coded card, which is needed when entering the building.

To date, approximately 1,348,000 men and 6,500 women have become members.

TRAINING HOURS

The Kodokan is open for training between 3:30 and 8:30 P.M., Monday through Saturday. It is closed on Sundays and national holidays, as well as during the New Year's vacation, that is, from December 29 through January 3.

INSTRUCTION

Members of the Kodokan pay a monthly fee and train at a time convenient to themselves. They receive instruction from accredited Kodokan instructors and high-ranking senior members of the Kodokan. In addition to regular classes, there is a school with a Men's Special Section, a Woman's Division and an International Division.

Special facilities are available to overseas members in the International Division, in which members are divided into four groups: Beginners, Class A, Class B and Special. International Division instructors have all lived abroad and are familiar with the needs of foreign students.

JUDO MAGAZINE

The Kodokan publishes *Judo*, a magazine which serves as the official organ of the All Japan Judo Federation. Correspondence concerning subscriptions should be sent to the Kodokan Editorial Department.

ANNUAL EVENTS

The main annual event is *Kagami-biraki*, which marks the reopening of the dojo after the New Year's vacation and the start of winter training (*kangeiko*).

The National Upper Division Tournament and the All Japan Championships are held in April. Other events include the Spring Red and White Tournament in May, Midsummer Training in July, the All Japan Women's Championships in September and the Autumn Red and White Tournament held in October. Examinations for advancement in grade are held monthly.

Glossary

shizen hontai, basic natural posture, 37
shizentai, natural posture, 37
shomen, front, 148
shomen-zuke, pistol at the abdomen, 202
sode-guruma-jime, sleeve wheel choke, 123
sode-tori, sleeve grab, 182
sode-tsurikomi-goshi, sleeve lift-pull hip throw, 71
so-katsu, composite method, 254
Sotai Renshu, joint exercises, 247
soto-makikomi, outer wraparound throw, 90
suigetsu, solar plexus, 138
sukui-nage, scooping throw, 87
sumi-gaeshi, corner throw, 84
sumi-otoshi, corner drop, 98
suri-age, forehead thrust, 176
sutemi-waza, sacrifice techniques, 55

tachiai, standing techniques, 146
tachi-waza, standing techniques, 55
tai, ready posture, 224
taijutsu, jujutsu, 15
tai-otoshi, body drop, 73
tai-sabaki, body control, 39
taka-geri, high front kick, 243
taki-otoshi, waterfall drop, 232
tanden-katsu, lower abdomen method, 252
Tandoku Renshu, individual exercises, 240
tani-otoshi, valley drop, 85
tate-shiho-gatame, straight locking four-corner hold, 116
te-gatame, hand armlock, 195
tegatana-ate, knife hand strikes, 58
tendo, bregma, 138
te-waza, hand techniques, 55
tomoe-nage, circular throw, 82
tori, taker, 59
tsubame-gaeshi, swallow counter, 103
tsugi-ashi, moving with one foot leading, the other following, 39
tsukiage, uppercut, 183
tsukidashi, hand thrust, 137
tsuki-kake, see *tsukkake*.
tsukkake, punch, 175
tsukkomi, thrust, 178
tsukkomi-jime, thrust choke, 124
tsukuri, positioning for throw, 44
tsurigane, testicles, 138
tsuri-goshi, lifting hip throw, 77
tsurikomi, lifting and pulling, 81
tsurikomi-goshi, lift-pull hip throw, 71

uchikudaki, smashing, 229
uchi-mata, inner thigh reaping throw, 75
uchi-mata-gaeshi, inner thigh reaping throw counter, 106
uchi-mata-makikomi, inner thigh wraparound throw, 108

uchi-mata-sukashi, inner thigh reaping throw slip, 102
uchioroshi, downward strike, 218
ude-ate, hand and arm strikes, 58
ude-garami, entangled armlock, 125
ude-gatame, armlock, 195
ude-hishigi-ashi-gatame, leg armlock, 129
ude-hishigi-hara-gatame, stomach armlock, 129
ude-hishigi-hiza-gatame, knee armlock, 128
ude-hishigi-juji-gatame, cross armlock, 126
ude-hishigi-sankaku-gatame, triangular armlock, 130
ude-hishigi-te-gatame, hand armlock, 130
ude-hishigi-ude-gatame, arm armlock, 127
ude-hishigi-waki-gatame, armpit armlock, 129
ude-waza, arm strikes, 55
ue-ate, upward blow, 241
uke, receiver, 59
ukemi, technique of falling safely, 45
uki-goshi, floating hip throw, 63
uki-otoshi, floating drop, 91
uki-waza, floating throw, 93
ura, back, 224
ura-nage, back throw, 97
ushiro-ate, rear strike, 240
ushiro-dori, hold from behind, 177
ushiro-eri-dori, collar hold from behind, 195
ushiro-geri, rear kick, 242
ushiro-goshi, back hip throw, 96
ushiro-jime, choke from behind, 195
ushiro-sumi-tsuki, rear-corner blow, 246
ushiro-tsuki, back blow, 136
ushiro-tsuki-mae-shita-tsuke, rear/downward blows, 247
ushiro-uchi, rear blow, 246
uto, nasion, 138
utsuri-goshi, hip shift, 88

waki-gatame, armpit armlock, 174

yawara, jujutsu, 15
yoko-ate, side body drop, 99
yoko-gake, side body drop, 99
yoko-geri, side kick, 198
yoko-guruma, side wheel, 95
yoko-otoshi, side drop, 78
yoko-shiho-gatame, side locking four-corner hold, 115
yoko-sutemi-waza, side sacrifice techniques, 55
yoko-tsuki, thrust to side, 180
yoko-uchi, side blow, 176
yoko-wakare, side separation, 94
yubisaki-ate, fingertip strikes, 58
yudachi, shower, 232
yukiore, snowbreak, 236
yume-no-uchi, dreaming, 226

zengo-tsuki, front-rear strikes, 244

Index